# CONSTITUTIONAL REFORM

Geraint Thomas
LSE  Jan 2002.

# CONSTITUTIONAL REFORM

RODNEY BRAZIER

SECOND EDITION

Oxford University Press · Oxford
1998

Oxford University Press, Great Clarendon Street, Oxford OX2 6DP
Oxford New York
Athens Auckland Bangkok Bogota Bombay
Buenos Aires Calcutta Cape Town Dar es Salaam
Delhi Florence Hong Kong Istanbul Karachi
Kuala Lumpur Madras Madrid Melbourne
Mexico City Nairobi Paris Singapore
Taipei Tokyo Toronto Warsaw
and associated companies in
Berlin Ibadan

Oxford is a trade mark of Oxford University Press

Published in the United States
by Oxford University Press Inc., New York

British Library Cataloguing in Publication Data
Data available

Library of Congress Cataloging in Publication Data
Data available
ISBN 0–19–876524–X
ISBN 0–19–876523–1 (Pbk)

1 3 5 7 9 10 8 6 4 2

Typeset by Hope Services (Abingdon) Ltd.
Printed in Great Britain
on acid-free paper by
Biddles Ltd., Guildford and King's Lynn

# Preface

THE purpose of this new edition remains the same as for the original book, which was published in 1991. It examines the shortcomings of the British constitution and proposes an agenda for reform. The weaknesses in that constitution are widely understood: accordingly, the emphasis throughout the book remains on suggesting practical improvements rather than, once again, rehearsing what is wrong with British constitutional law and practice.

Since the first edition was published constitutional reform has moved from the fringes of national debate to its centre. Before the 1990s demands for constitutional change were largely confined to a variegated collection of people—the political heirs of the Liberal Party, some academics, a few think-tanks, a few sturdy individuals, and even the occasional judge. But from a practical point of view what has changed since 1990 is that the momentum for constitutional reform which had steadily built up through the Thatcher years was welcomed by the Labour Party. Today, the Labour Government has in its hands the power to put its many constitutional plans into effect. To reflect those developments I have added a new chapter which explains why and how Labour's attitude to the constitution changed and what its constitutional policies are. Details of particular changes which the Labour Government wishes to implement are given in that chapter and (where appropriate) are developed in later chapters. This particular conversion of the Labour Party was unforeseeable in 1990, and some of the pessimism over the prospects for change which were expressed in the first edition of this book has proved, happily, to have been misplaced. But I wish to stress that this is not a book designed to react to the constitutional agenda of any one party or group. Indeed, a major theme remains that of examining the methodology of reform, an important consideration that has, in the main, been shunned by all the political parties. In my view the state of the British constitution, and the manner in which it is revised, are matters of such overarching importance that new processes are still needed to carry forward reform in a considered, coherent, and comprehensive way. Those processes are described in this book.

As well as adding another chapter, I have expanded the Bibliography so that the reader has full access to sources which will be of help in further reading. I am grateful to the publishers of the *Northern Ireland Legal Quarterly* and of *Public Law* for permission to use articles which originally appeared in those journals as the bases for Chapters 2, 3, and 9. I also thank students who have been members of my classes on Constitutional Reform for the intellectual stimulation which they have (perhaps unwittingly) given me.

R.B.

*University of Manchester*
*January 1998*

# Contents

1. The Limits of Reform                           1
2. The Way Forward                               16
3. Labour and the Constitution                   38
4. Parliamentary Democracy                       56
5. The Second-Chamber Paradox                    85
6. Ministerial Powers                           103
7. A Constitutional Guiding Light               126
8. Defending Rights                             144
9. Government, Law, and Judges                  162

*Bibliography*                                  183

*Index*                                         187

# 1 The Limits of Reform

THE United Kingdom shares with Israel alone in the developed world the eccentricity of not having a written constitution.[1] For many people this state of affairs is at the root of what has gone seriously wrong in British constitutional law and practice. If they are right I believe that other remedies must be found, because a written British constitution may be unattainable.

## A Fundamental Limitation

Constitutions have, of course, been granted or adopted for many different reasons. New constitutions have marked stages in a progression towards self-government (as in most British colonies before independence); they have established a system of government in a newly independent state (as in the United States of America in 1787), or in a reconstituted state (such as Malaysia in 1963 or Tanzania in 1964 or Germany on reunification in 1990); they have marked a major change in the system of government (as in Spain in 1978); they have been adopted in order to rebuild the machinery of government following defeat in war (as in the Federal Republic of Germany in 1949); and they have declared a new beginning after a revolution, or after the collapse of a regime (as in France in 1791 and in 1958). None of these factors has operated in Britain. There has been no military invasion since 1066. True, there were two revolutions in the seventeenth century, but their effects were limited. The Civil War of 1642–8 led to the execution of the King and to a republican Commonwealth—but it was followed by the restoration of the monarchy in 1660. The second revolution, of 1688–9, forced the abdication of James II, gave the Crown to a usurper, changed the line of succession to the throne, and, through the Bill of Rights of

---

[1] New Zealand abandoned that state of affairs when she adopted a Constitution Act in 1986.

1689, restricted the royal prerogative in important respects—but Parliament made no greater attempts than that to restate the constitution. Constitutions had not become fashionable at that time. The union of England and Scotland in 1707, and of Great Britain and Ireland in 1800, produced rudimentary frameworks of a written constitution, but nothing more sophisticated. This sweep of history has tended to confirm British insularity and its general lack of concern for the constitutional experience of other states.

As a result, while a citizen in almost any state of the world may obtain a copy of the constitution of his country, a British citizen has to seek out his constitution in a bewildering number of places and forms—legislation, judicial decisions, statements about the royal prerogative and constitutional conventions, the law and practice of Parliament, European Community law, the internal rules of the political parties, and so on. It is scarcely surprising if he is tempted to take a short cut by traversing the pages of literature on the British constitution published by authoritative writers, and writers who aspire to be authoritative. Now it is true that the student of a written constitution must read beyond its text in order to understand the government of his country. In the United States, for instance, he could read the Constitution in less than half an hour, but he would then have to immerse himself in the law reports to see what fuller meaning had been given to it by the Supreme Court, and he would have to take account of a number of non-legal glosses which have been set upon the Constitution, primarily by convention. Even so, that is an easier task than the one which faces the scholar of the British constitution. Why, then, despite the absence of the kind of national emergency which has propelled other states into constitution-writing has no British government proposed a written constitution for the United Kingdom? There are several reasons, but I suggest that one is of overriding importance: in foreseeable political circumstances there will be no cross-party agreement either about the principle of a written constitution or about its most important features.

Major constitutional change in Britain during this century has often been preceded by agreement between the Government and the Opposition—or at least by an attempt to reach such agreement. So,

for instance, the Ulster crisis before the First World War led to discussions between Asquith and Bonar Law to try to produce a better
understanding of the respective Liberal and Unionist positions,
although in the event a common policy proved impossible to achieve.
Again, during the abdication crisis in 1936 Baldwin consulted the
Leader of the Opposition and the Leader of the Liberal Party about
the King's plan to marry Mrs Simpson, with the result that all the
political leaders agreed that Edward VIII's abdication must take
place before the marriage. At various times during this century
attempts to reform the House of Lords have been accompanied by
inter-party negotiations, almost culminating in complete accord on
reform between the Labour, Conservative, and Liberal Parties in
1968. And the Prime Minister and the Leader of the Opposition
have sought to maintain a degree of consensus on constitutional
matters in Northern Ireland over the past thirty years. Such cross-
party co-operation is not, it is true, always looked for in constitutional affairs—it was not, for example, sought when the Labour
Government tried to devolve power to Scotland and Wales in the
late 1970s, and the present Labour Government is proceeding with
its constitutional reform programme without seeking agreement with
the Conservative Party on it.[2] But it is fair to describe cross-party
discussions as a frequent characteristic of constitutional developments of the highest importance. Nothing less would be needed for
any attempt to introduce a written constitution. Multi-party agreement would endow the resulting document with enormous political
legitimacy and durability. Even if it were bolstered by acceptance at
a referendum, a constitution enacted on the strength of a
Government's parliamentary majority in the teeth of Opposition
protests could not be considered as necessarily permanent.
Amendments would probably be sought after a change of government, and that process could, theoretically, continue indefinitely if
the area of dispute were great enough. The risk of such instability,
however, should not be exaggerated, as an illustration from France

[2] Before coming to power, however, the Labour Party did conclude an agreement on a
complete package of constitutional changes with the Liberal Democrats, and Mr Tony
Blair has set up a Cabinet committee with their representatives on it to take those reforms
forward: see Ch. 3.

shows. The Constitution of the Fifth French Republic of 1958 was drafted largely on the wishes of Charles de Gaulle in a constituent assembly dominated by the political parties of the right. The Socialists and Communists, who opposed the draft, were in a minority in the assembly, and they subsequently campaigned against endorsement of the draft in a national referendum. The French people did endorse the Constitution: but when the Socialist François Mitterrand was elected President of the Republic some twenty years later he made no attempt to alter the fundamentals of the Gaullist Constitution (which endows the President with considerable power).[3] Perhaps the opponents of a newly written British constitution would accept defeat gracefully if that was the people's wish; but not necessarily: it would all depend on how deep the disagreements were and how determined those opponents were to get their version adopted. While the manner of adoption of the French Constitution provides one possible model for a United Kingdom in which the main political parties did not agree on the main provisions of a new written constitution, it would be second-best to a process which sought as wide a degree of consensus as possible on such a dramatic constitutional change. Indeed, that will be a major theme of this book.

In the vast majority of developed states the constitution is the supreme law: it designates the principal organs of government, and gives them their authority. It is normally also a kind of higher law: all, or some, of the rules set out in the constitution are hierarchically superior to other laws and are only alterable by a specially prescribed procedure. In a number of countries the courts are given jurisdiction by the constitution to declare invalid laws which are inconsistent with the constitution. Even if a new British constitution could not as a matter of law be entrenched in those ways (a point which will not be dwelt on now[4]), it would have to set out and to delimit the relative powers of national and local government, the legislature, and the judiciary. A written constitution—at least, one whose text had achieved some degree of cross-party consensus—would presumably acquire a degree of entrenchment in practice, even if not in law, for

---

[3] See John Bell, *French Constitutional Law* (Oxford: Clarendon Press, 1992), ch. 1.

[4] Questions about entrenchment will be addressed in Ch. 8.

a government would risk massive criticism if it sought unilaterally to amend for its own purposes a new constitutional settlement. This would impede the complete freedom of action traditionally enjoyed by the British government to carry out its policies. No government would wish to do that; any Opposition hopes to be the Government one fine day, and so would not want it to be done, either; as a result—at least until recently—both the Conservative and Labour Parties, whether in or out of government, have opposed the idea of a written constitution. They do so, perhaps, from an entirely honourable motive, namely, that the policies placed before the voters at a general election should be put into place by Parliament and Ministers as soon as may be once those policies have been approved by the electorate: there should, therefore, be no law to stand in the way of the popular will democratically expressed. Now an analysis such as that begs a number of questions which will be addressed in later chapters, but it is a political fact that such an analysis is adhered to. To expect the main political parties voluntarily to accept such a wide-ranging limitation on their power to enact manifesto commitments would be to ask for a self-denying ordinance of breathtaking proportions.[5]

A separate political obstacle to the enactment of a written constitution for the United Kingdom is that, despite the advanced age of the British constitution, there is disagreement about some of its provisions. Such disagreement sometimes divides the political parties. One important example concerns the return of a hung Parliament. Before each of the general elections in 1979, 1983, 1987, and 1992, some commentators anticipated, as did the smaller parties, the election of a House of Commons in which no party had a majority. In the event all were disappointed, so two key questions did not have to be answered. One was whether the Conservative and Labour Parties were correct in believing that the largest party in such a House is entitled to form a minority government, or whether the smaller parties were nearer the mark in insisting that a coalition should be sought first. The other question was whether (as the two

---

[5] In opposition the Labour Party appeared to soften its attitude to the possibility of an eventual written constitution, but no more of that has been heard so far in government: see Ch. 3.

main parties thought) a Prime Minister at the head of a minority government is automatically entitled to a dissolution of Parliament at any time of his choosing, or whether (as the smaller parties maintained) a dissolution might only be granted by the Queen if another government could not be formed from the existing House. It would be surprising if the political parties, having failed over the years to reach agreement about what the constitution ordains in such circumstances—and in several others as well—were suddenly to achieve such a consensus for the purpose of adopting a written constitution which neither of the two main parties really wanted in the first place.

The prospects for a written constitution based on multi-party support are even gloomier when attention is turned to its possible main provisions. No constitution would be worth having if it failed to provide for such matters as the composition and powers of the legislature, the manner of choosing its members, and the structure of government and administration away from the centre. These are the very matters which have divided the political parties over the years and which would have to be examined afresh. That would almost certainly frustrate the whole enterprise. There would be no agreement about the future of the House of Lords. The Conservative Party champions the status quo; the Labour Party wishes to replace it with an elected second chamber with limited powers; the Liberal Democrats want an elected chamber with major and general legislative authority. The large measure of all-party agreement on House of Lords reform which was achieved in 1968 has been shattered.[6] Then there would be total disagreement about the structure of regional government in the United Kingdom. Further devolution to Scotland and Wales is opposed by the Conservatives, whereas it is being carried forward by the other two parties; the Liberal Democrats are the more ambitious, seeking a pattern of national and regional governments within a federal structure for the United Kingdom. The appropriate balance of power between Parliament and existing local authorities, too, would split the parties. The present scheme, largely set by the late Conservative Government in favour of Westminster and to the detriment of county and district

[6] See Ch. 5.

councils, is not accepted by the other two parties, which wish to see a return of power to the localities. Lastly, the system on which elections to the House of Commons should be based in a reformed constitution would obviously cause fierce political argument. The existing first-past-the-post system is stoutly defended by the Conservatives, who are convinced that any other system would produce weak governments. Proportional representation is demanded by the Liberal Democrats. Labour is still wedded to the present rules, although the Government has established a commission to prepare for a national referendum on the electoral system.[7] The Labour Party has recognized the advantages of proportional representation by proposing it for elections to its planned new second chamber and for its proposed Scottish, Welsh, and English regional authorities, and for elections to the European Parliament. Conservative and Labour negotiators in any forum which might discuss a new British constitution might accept the first-past-the-post model as the lowest common denominator, but the Liberal Democrats would be outraged, some Labour people would not accept the question as settled, and many outside the political parties would continue to view that system as fundamentally unfair.

This diversity of approach would block the adoption of a written constitution. It derives from the realities of the political situation and it would ruin any attempt to proceed with such a massively ambitious project, at least if it were to be preceded by multi-party agreement or even grudging acquiescence. In effect it represents a fundamental limitation on the possible scope of constitutional reform in the United Kingdom.

For the sake of completeness I should add that there would be no obstacle to the writing of a British constitution as a result of purely drafting difficulties. At least three versions have already been written.[8]

---

[7] See Ch. 3.

[8] See generally R. Brazier, 'Enacting a Constitution' [1992] *Statute Law Review* 104; and for specific drafts see Tony Benn's Commonwealth of Britain Bill (HC Bill 161 (1990–1)); Institute of Public Policy Research, *A Written Constitution for the United Kingdom* (London: Mansell, 1993).

## Diagnoses and Prescriptions

As confidence in Victorian England was moving towards its zenith Charles Dickens published *Our Mutual Friend*. In it, Mr Podsnap (enunciating clearly, for he was addressing a foreigner) said: 'We Englishmen are Very Proud of our Constitution, Sir. It was Bestowed Upon Us By Providence. No Other Country is so Favoured as This Country.' Podsnap concluded, regretfully no doubt, that foreign countries were 'a mistake'.[9] Men of affairs, including the great contemporary writers on the constitution, agreed with Podsnap's sentiments—at least in so far as they lauded the advantages of the Victorian constitution. As Empire gave way to Commonwealth, the general view in Britain that the Westminster constitution was near perfect encouraged successive governments to endow newly independent states with versions of it (although there were remarkable differences, such as, occasionally, a federal structure and, usually, a Bill of Rights). This pride provided a further disincentive to learn anything of a constitutional nature from abroad. But doubts about the British constitution emerged in the 1960s and grew through the following decades, until today it seems that few people (usually Conservatives) have anything much to say for the poor old thing. What has gone wrong in just forty years?

It is fashionable to ascribe most of the blame to Mrs Margaret Thatcher.[10] On this view, the subtle balance of powers in the constitution was totally thrown out by her imperious premiership. As Prime Minister she ruthlessly seized and shifted levers of power which her predecessors either left untouched or used with restraint. Those Ministers who were not 'one of us' were sacked, and others more congenial were put in their places; the disbursement of patronage, and the winning of general elections, kept backbenchers to heel; she interfered to an unprecedented extent in Ministers' departmental responsibilities; she reduced the collective authority of the Cabinet, and ruled through Cabinet committees or (more frequently)

---

[9] C. Dickens, *Our Mutual Friend* (London, 1865), ch. xi.

[10] See, e.g. P. McAuslan and J. F. McEldowney (eds.), *Law, Legitimacy and the Constitution* (London: Sweet & Maxwell, 1985); K. Ewing and C. Gearty, *Freedom under Thatcher: Civil Liberties in Modern Britain* (Oxford: Clarendon Press, 1990).

through hand-picked, informal groups of Ministers; in the Cabinet system, in short, she made herself first above inferiors. She manipulated the press, she cut down the authority of other centres of power, such as local councils, she elbowed aside inconvenient civil liberties, she politicized the senior civil service. As with all good caricatures, there is much truth in that sketch. But even if it were an entirely accurate reflection of Mrs Thatcher's effect on the constitution, that would be a poor basis on which to deconstruct and reconstruct it. Mrs Thatcher was not immortal. Mr John Major reverted to more traditional forms: Mr Tony Blair gives the impression of preferring a more presidential style. But to construct a new constitutional edifice solely as a response to any one Prime Minister's mode of governance would be misguided. That said, there are wholly undesirable features of the British constitution which pre-dated Mrs Thatcher's accession and which survived her resignation.

When Lord Hailsham coined his chilling phrase 'elective dictatorship',[11] Mrs Thatcher had only just been elected Leader of the Opposition. He was describing a Labour Government, returned by a minority of the electorate, which (he claimed) was able to legislate as it wished on whatever it wished—even to bring about, as Labour had promised, irreversible changes in society—because no external restraints existed to stop it from doing so. This was dictatorship, tempered only by the requirement of fighting regular general elections, but dictatorship nonetheless. When that Labour Government was rejected in 1979 and Lord Hailsham became Mrs Thatcher's Lord Chancellor, we heard no more from him about this awful spectre. Yet the elective dictatorship of the 1970s survived and prospered in the 1980s: indeed, there were examples of changes brought about in that latter decade, such as privatization, which were truly irreversible in a way in which no policy of the late Labour Government had been irreversible. Party discipline among Conservative Members of Parliament, underpinned by the loyalty to Mrs Thatcher which her remarkable general election victories engendered, meant that Bills were, on the whole, passed at the Government's request, utterly unhindered by any entrenched laws

[11] See Lord Hailsham, *The Dilemma of Democracy* (London: Collins, 1978), 9–11.

or rights beyond the reach of Parliament. The Conservative administration's opponents often cite a long list of its Acts and actions which they label as authoritarian, undemocratic, and illiberal and which would have been difficult (and in some cases impossible) to pass or to take in any other western democracy which enjoys special constitutional guarantees. While reasonable people can hold different views about the necessity or desirability of some of that Government's measures, the ease with which they—and, it must be stressed, those of earlier governments—have been translated into law or administrative practice is very worrying.

Members of Parliament had abdicated parliamentary sovereignty in favour of elective dictatorship long before Mrs Thatcher became Prime Minister. The House of Commons has allowed the power over the Crown which it had secured in earlier times to be usurped, without a fight, by the government. Not every administration will take full advantage of elective dictatorship, but that is not the point: the fundamental objection is that such a dictatorship has come to pass, and the powers which it confers can be exercised at will at any time. Indeed, how much more convincing today—and how much more disturbing—is Walter Bagehot's characterization of the House of Commons as an electoral college which chooses the government.[12] Today that is its primary function, and it is one which, thanks to party cohesiveness, is accomplished on election night when one party has secured a majority of seats. In this modern elective dictatorship, once the Commons has been used as an indirect electoral college its members are content, on the whole, to take their orders. Catalogues of reasons have been compiled explaining why this has happened, and certainly things like the growth of the party and whip system, based on inducements and threats, have contributed mightily. Common to all those reasons, however, is one factor: the supine manner in which Members of Parliament have allowed successive Prime Ministers (including, it may be said, Mr Blair) to benefit from elective dictatorship. Nowadays few would dispute that the powers of the Prime Minister have increased, are increasing, and ought to be diminished. The remedy is in Members' own hands. They can

---

[12] See W. Bagehot, *The English Constitution* (first pub., 1867; London: Fontana, 1963), 157–8.

curb prime-ministerial authority with their voices and, if necessary, with their votes—a point which will be developed in later chapters. If they choose not to act in this way, it is little wonder that others canvass constitutional reforms in order to redress the balance of power.

This abdication of power to the government has been helped by a reverence for antiquity which in large part accounts for the anti-quated state of the House of Commons. It is right to have regard to wisdom from the past, to respect earlier achievements, and to recognize and to preserve the best in an evolutionary system of government. Yet if a Member of Parliament who had been elected at one of the 1910 general elections could return today, how much would be entirely familiar to him in the House of Commons, despite all that had changed in Britain and the world in the meantime! The chamber looks the same (carefully restored to its original design after a direct hit by a bomb in the Second World War), although he would be surprised to see 120 women Members. The House sits for broadly the same period in each year, and still conducts some of its business under, as it were, cover of darkness, although there is more committee work, conducted in the mornings as well as later in the day. The absence of any effective scrutiny of government taxation and borrowing policy, the very limited scope and time for legislative initiatives by backbenchers, the shortage of working (as distinct from club) facilities, the intolerance shown by the two major parties towards smaller ones—all these would be recognized almost as old friends by an Edwardian visitor. Yet the vast increases in governmental responsibilities and in the volume of primary and secondary legislation, and the changes in society which have all occurred since his time, might have led him to expect that the House would have transformed itself to meet these new challenges. In the main, it has not done so.[13]

As concerns about the accretion of governmental power have grown, the shortcomings of other institutions and the absence of countervailing safeguards have become more apparent. The House of Lords cannot be expected to challenge the might of elected dicta-

---

[13] The Labour Government has, however, set up a select committee on the modernization of House of Commons procedures. See also Ch. 4.

torship, for its authority has long been limited by convention and by law. It has proved a significant inconvenience for Labour governments and an irritant for Conservative governments, but it lacks both legal power and political authority to do much more. The judges have tried to meet the challenges thrown up by aspects of elective dictatorship, not least through judicial review, but they can only work with the raw materials supplied to them by the law. There is no higher or special law which the judiciary could enforce in order to strike a balance between, on the one hand, the executive and the legislature, and, on the other, the rights of the citizen. Those rights which the citizen does have can be restricted or abolished by ordinary legislation. While the Labour Government is to incorporate the European Convention on Human Rights into municipal law this will be done in a way so as to preserve parliamentary sovereignty.

All this, and more, has led to demands for constitutional reform. The nostrums which have been suggested include the introduction of proportional representation for elections to the House of Commons, a Bill of Rights, an elected replacement for the House of Lords, devolution of power, and a written constitution. Such calls have come from a variety of sources, and the detailed prescriptions will be considered in this book. A number of extra-parliamentary bodies have carried the torch of reform. For example, Charter 88 is an all-party and non-party campaign for major constitutional reconstruction. It demands the adoption of a new constitutional settlement which would incorporate electoral reform, an elected second chamber, and a Bill of Rights, all enshrined in a written constitution. The Institute of Public Policy Research, too, has worked on the case for, and the shape of, a new constitutional settlement.[14] The Liberal Democrats are continuing the struggle for radical change begun many years ago by the Liberal Party, including proposals for the introduction of proportional representation, an elected upper house, devolution of power, and a Bill of Rights; the adoption of a written constitution is envisaged in the long term. The incorporation of the European Convention on Human Rights would be, for the Liberal

---

[14] See n. 8 above. The Constitution Unit (on which see Ch. 3) has been more concerned with the ways in which changes could be implemented, rather than with the merits or otherwise of particular reforms.

Democrats, an important remedy for constitutional ills, as would the enactment of extensive and detailed legislation to secure or improve other rights, such as those relating to equal opportunities, a non-discriminatory immigration policy, freedom of information, privacy, and press protection.[15] The Labour Party's constitutional policy underwent a sea-change in opposition, and because the Labour Government has the ability to change the British constitution as we approach the millennium and indeed beyond it, a separate chapter is devoted to that policy.[16] Particular reforms will be considered in appropriate chapters in this book. In summary, however, Labour's programme[17] envisages devolution of power to Scotland, Wales, and the regions of England, the reform of the House of Lords (first removing the hereditary peers, then instituting an elected second chamber), a referendum on the voting system for the House of Commons, freedom of information legislation, the incorporation into domestic law of the European Convention on Human Rights, and possibly a new system for appointing judges. In short, the Labour Government assumed office in May 1997 committed to more constitutional change than any previous administration.

The Conservative Party is completely out of step. Mrs Thatcher refused to join in the march towards a constitutional utopia. Her view was that Britain's constitution continues to serve the nation well, and that it allows the citizen to enjoy the greatest degree of liberty that is compatible with the rights of others and with the vital interests of the state. Moreover, Mrs Thatcher declared, her government would not consider any constitutional reform unless it were widely understood and supported in Parliament and in the country. Mr Major wedded himself to that policy, for soon after becoming Prime Minister he said in answer to a parliamentary question that he had no immediate plans for constitutional reform.[18] He maintained that position throughout his premiership, and indeed made the defence of the status quo a vital plank in his 1992 general election

---

[15] These proposals are set out in *Here We Stand*: *Proposals for Modernizing Britain's Democracy*, Liberal Democrat Federal White Paper No. 6 (London, 1993).

[16] See Ch. 3.

[17] See *A New Agenda for Democracy* (London: Labour Party, 1993); *New Labour*: *Because Britain Deserves Better* (London: Labour Party, 1997).

[18] 182 HC Debs. 1107 (13 Dec. 1990).

campaign. One of his last speeches as Prime Minister confirmed his stance.[19] We can only wait and see whether Mr William Hague will move the Conservative Party any nearer to the positions taken by the other two main parties.


## The Bases of Reform

In this book, I am going to base my consideration of British constitutional reform on a number of precepts. One has already been mentioned, and will be developed in the next chapter: major constitutional upheaval should be based on the ideal of consensus, so that as far as possible multi-party agreement should precede it. The state of the constitution is a matter of overarching importance in the country's affairs and should not be the exclusive preserve of the party which happens to be the government. A second precept is that the traditional notions upon which the constitution of the United Kingdom is predicated are worth continuing (or, as the case may be, restoring) and making more effective. In summary, these are that the United Kingdom is a liberal democracy which enjoys a regularly-elected representative legislature, a rough separation of powers, a government limited in its authority partly by the rule of law and partly by convention, and an independent judiciary. The value of those notions is, to me, self-evident. A third precept is what I will term constitutional propriety, which is a notion that should condition what governments do. It is generally accepted that the actors in the British constitution—and principally Ministers—should exercise their undoubted legal powers with restraint. This is what A. V. Dicey termed limited government: the government's powers, derived from the law, are (or should be) used in such a way that what it does, and how it does it, respects certain values. Elective dictatorship is inimical to such an idea of constitutional propriety—at least if governments take full advantage of what they are given by that dictatorship. Of course, there are difficulties with a principle of constitutional propriety. Who is to say what is constitutionally

[19] 290 HC Debs. 1055–66 (20 Feb. 1997). For his Lord Chancellor's support see 573 HL Debs. 1449–56 (3 July 1996).

appropriate? Different politicians may well take various views; the Government may claim propriety while the Opposition denies it. Proof of a breach of propriety in such circumstances will be impossible. But a notion of constitutional propriety has some worth. It can provide guidelines for action, even if they are mainly of a negative kind. It would, for example, clearly be wrong for the government to procure the enactment of legislation subversive of the democratic basis of the constitution, or to enact retrospective criminal laws, or to confiscate property without compensation, or to abolish access to the courts, or to pack the courts with members of the government party prepared to do Ministers' bidding. It would be helpful if a mechanism could be devised through which politicians could work towards a fuller explanation of limited government, or constitutional propriety, and a mechanism which could do this as a small part of its purpose will be suggested in the next chapter.

Before any particular constitutional problem is analysed against that background with a view to seeing how it might be resolved, a very important practical question must be addressed. It involves the appropriate methodology of constitutional reform in the United Kingdom, and it will be considered in Chapter 2.

# 2 The Way Forward

WHAT I want to consider in this chapter is not the case for any given constitutional change, but a logically prior set of questions about altering the British constitution. What machinery exists for bringing about changes? Is that machinery satisfactory? Is there any relevant experience from overseas which shows how things might be better ordered in the United Kingdom? In the light of answers to those questions, might there be any better model through which revisions could be carried out in this country?

## Reaction and Reform

Governments and Oppositions have so much confidence in the right-ness of their general policy proposals that they usually include them in their election manifestos without obtaining any independent assessments of them, and without testing public opinion. That is the traditional British way: the victors of the ensuing election point to the electors' assumed approval of their manifesto as authority for what they wish to do as a government. Policies affecting the consti-tution, however, sometimes have not even featured in election manifestos: they have been formulated as governments have gone along. Just occasionally, it is true, constitutional matters have been mentioned in manifestos: recent examples include the Conservative pledge at the 1983 election to abolish the Greater London Council and the metropolitan county councils, and Labour's promise at the October 1974 election to introduce devolution of government to Scotland and Wales. And, of course, the present Government did set out the substance of its constitutional reform programme in the party's 1997 general election manifesto.[1] This was exceptional: changes to the British constitution have tended to have been under-taken in the past in response to events.

[1] See Ch. 3.

This reluctance on the part of governments to preface possible changes to the constitution by detailed analysis of the problems, and by consultation of those likely to be affected by them, is not the result of any lack of available means. On the contrary, a wide range of methods has, historically, been relied on, which may conveniently be summarized in three groups. The first consists of departmental committees of inquiry and Royal Commissions. Their common features are that the people conducting them are expected to hold hearings, ascertain facts, make findings and put forward recommendations. The human resources devoted to such investigations—often far more than could be spared within the four walls of any government department—should result in a well-researched, informative, and non-partisan report. In this century, there are many instances of the use of departmental committees to inquire into constitutional matters—for example, the Donoughmore Committee on Ministers' Powers, the Masterman and Armitage Committees on the Political Activities of Civil Servants, the Franks Committee on Administrative Tribunals and Inquiries, the Fulton Committee on the Civil Service, the Franks Committee on Section 2 of the Official Secrets Act 1911, the Radcliffe Committee on Ministerial Memoirs, and the Scott Inquiry into Arms to Iraq.[2] Royal Commissions, too, have been appointed to inquiry into aspects of the constitution: in this century, two Commissions have considered the electoral system, in 1910 and again in 1918; three have pondered the civil service; one has investigated abuses of the honours system, one has inquired into tribunals of inquiry, and one has explored devolution—the famously misnamed Royal Commission on the Constitution.[3] Only one Royal Commission (on criminal justice) was appointed by the 1979 Conservative Government, which preferred to formulate policy through private, internal reviews of issues by Ministers and civil servants, followed by the publication of proposals and subsequently by legislation. Such a method has the advantage for Ministers that they

[2] See respectively Cmd. 4060 (1932); Cmd. 7718 (1949); Cmnd. 7057 (1970); Cmnd. 218 (1957); Cmnd. 3638 (1968); Cmnd. 5104 (1972); Cmnd. 6368 (1976); HC 115 (1995–6).
[3] See respectively Cd. 5163 (1910); Cd. 9044 (1918); Cd. 7852 (1915); Cmd. 3909 (1931); Cmd. 9613 (1955); Cmd. 1789 (1922); Cmnd. 3121 (1966); Cmnd. 5460 (1973).

will not be presented with proposals that are politically unacceptable, but it has disadvantages for the public interest which will be considered later.

Occasionally a government wishes to seek cross-party support for constitutional initiatives, or at least to try to reduce the area of disagreement between the parties. In that case it will tend to look to a second group of consultative devices which embraces talks on Privy Councillor terms, more formal inter-party talks, and Speaker's Conferences. The Prime Minister may invite the Leader of the Opposition to accept briefings from the government, or to discuss policy options with him, on condition that information communicated is not revealed to others without the Prime Minister's consent. In the constitutional sphere, the examples this century have been Asquith's meetings with Bonar Law on Ulster in 1913, Baldwin's talks with MacDonald on the government of India in 1927, his consultation of Attlee (and, for the Liberals, Sinclair) on the abdication crisis in 1936, and the talks since the early 1970s between various Prime Ministers and Opposition Leaders on Northern Ireland. Only the pre-First World War initiative on Ulster was a complete failure; the others achieved a remarkable degree of political agreement. However, the total number of occasions giving rise to constitutional talks on Privy Councillor terms has obviously been small. Reform of the House of Lords has been the subject of formal, inter-party talks on a number of occasions, the last of which took place before the introduction of the Parliament (No. 2) Bill in 1968. Almost full agreement was reached between the parties in that forum before the Government broke off the talks in retaliation for the rejection by the House of Lords of the Southern Rhodesia (United Nations Sanctions) Order. Speaker's Conferences have examined various aspects of electoral law on five occasions in the last sixty years. The Conferences consist of Members of Parliament from all sides of the House of Commons, nominated by the parties themselves and formally appointed by the Speaker, who chairs the Conferences. A limitation on the efficacy of Speaker's Conferences is, however, that they are only set up at the instigation of the Prime Minister. They have no powers, such as those enjoyed by select committees, other than to make recommendations. Decisions are sometimes arrived at by votes, which have sometimes been cast along party lines. While the recommendations of Speaker's Conferences are bound to be treated with respect, Prime Ministers have tended only to refer to them technical points of election law and procedure rather than wider issues of principle.

The Labour Government in 1997 established a standing Joint Consultative Cabinet Committee with ministerial and Liberal Democrat representatives. This important initiative will be examined in the next chapter in the context of the development of Labour's constitutional policy.

Those two groups of constitutional reviews, involving investigations by the great and the good, or consultations with Opposition parties, both require the initiative of the Prime Minister. By contrast, the third group, comprising parliamentary committees, depends on a parliamentary initiative in which the government's wishes may be a factor but not a decisive one. House of Commons departmental select committees have conducted a number of investigations into constitutional issues which before 1979 would, generally speaking, have been carried out (if at all) by departmental committees of inquiry. The main inquiries of relevance here have resulted in the Treasury and Civil Service Committee's two reports on the relationships between Ministers and civil servants, the Home Affairs Committee's report on the redistribution of Commons seats, the Foreign Affairs Committee's report on the Single European Act, the Defence Committee's report on the Westland helicopter affair, and reports from the Treasury and Civil Service Committee and from the Defence Committee on the acceptance of appointments by former civil servants.[4] The Home Affairs Committee investigation into the Representation of the People Acts was indistinguishable in character from the type of inquiry previously conducted by a Speaker's Conference;[5] indeed, that Committee's existence may account for the fact that no such Conference has been appointed since 1977. The House of Lords, too, has brought careful analysis to bear on constitutional questions through its select committees, the

---

[4] See respectively HC 92 (1985–6); HC 62 (1986–7); HC 97 (1986–7); HC 442 (1985–6); HC 519 (1985–6); HC 302 (1983–4); HC 392 (1987–8).

[5] HC 32 (1982–3).

most notable of which has been the Select Committee on a Bill of Rights.[6]

The most intractable problem in the United Kingdom constitution is Northern Ireland. It is remarkable that there seems to have been no attempt since partition to seek detailed solutions to that problem by British Ministers and the British political parties meeting together in any of the forums just mentioned. Northern Ireland's constitution has been considered internally by Northern Irish politicians of all parties (through, for example, the Northern Ireland Assembly, the Constitutional Convention, and the Northern Ireland Forum and its associated all-party talks), by the Secretary of State for Northern Ireland and the Northern Ireland political parties on very many occasions, and by the United Kingdom and Irish governments, especially of late through the apparatus of the Anglo-Irish Agreement. But the British Government and the Opposition parties have not held systematic and detailed discussions together. A solution enjoying even the unanimous agreement of the British political parties would not last without broad acceptance in the province. But it is odd that the most acute problem of the United Kingdom's constitution has not been analysed in a forum in which all the British political parties were represented formally.

Constitutional law reform often requires legislation in the same way as any other type of law reform. But the established law reform bodies—the Law Commission and the Law Reform Committee— have had no part in shaping such legislation. Why is that? One reason is that both bodies can only act on a reference from the Lord Chancellor.[7] The government would have to be persuaded that any such reference would be appropriate, and there are several factors which would make constitutional law references inappropriate. Both bodies are composed entirely of lawyers, and indeed the Law Reform Committee has been concerned wholly with technical rules of law. While the Law Commission has had necessarily to tackle issues of social policy in some of its work, the Commissioners would probably claim no particular competence in constitutional affairs, which are to a large degree bound up with politics. Politicians, quite fairly,

---

[6] HL 176 (1977–8).     [7] Law Commissions Act 1965, s. 3.

consider themselves to be the experts on the state of the constitution, having opinions about it which are worth more than those of any law reform body. In any case, the Law Commission is hard-pressed by its current load, and it would not be feasible, even if it were sensible, for the Commission to be given a whole new area of difficult work. As a result, no aspect of constitutional law (as distinct from administrative law) has formed any part of the Law Commission's law reform programmes, and no specific constitutional law reference has been made.

Even without the help of the official law-reform bodies, there is clearly no shortage of mechanisms for bringing about constitutional change in the United Kingdom. What persuades Ministers to seek information or advice about constitutional affairs from outside government? While precise categorization is impossible, some half-dozen reasons may be discerned which have prompted governments to go beyond their membership and beyond the civil service for inquiry, analysis, and advice. First, the national gravity of a constitutional problem may require a national solution arrived at by as many of the political parties as possible. The invitation from Asquith to Bonar law to talk on Privy Councillor terms about Ulster in 1913 is the best example of that. In the nature of things, such an overture will not often be made from such an acute cause. Secondly, events might take place which require public explanations of what has happened (or what is alleged to have happened) and guidance (and perhaps new rules) for the future. Public disquiet or alarm often produce an irresistible demand for independent investigation and report. Occurrences such as those which led to the Royal Commissions on the Rebellion in Ireland and on Honours, the Donoughmore Committee on Ministers' Powers, the Falkland Islands Review, the Radcliffe Committee on Ministerial Memoirs, the Royal Commission on Standards of Conduct in Public Life, the Scott inquiry into arms to Iraq, and the Committee on Standards in Public Life can all be seen as instances of that process.[8] Thirdly, there might be pressure for constitutional change with which Ministers do not particularly sympathize but which might lead to serious loss of political support

---

[8] See respectively Cd. 8729 (1916); Cmd. 1789 (1922); Cmd. 4060 (1932); Cmnd. 8787 (1983); Cmnd. 6386 (1976); Cmnd. 6526 (1976); HC 115 (1995–6); Cm. 2850 (1995).

for the government if it were to reject the case for reform out of hand. Ministers might decide that an official inquiry would be the least of all evils; in setting one up the government would be seen to be doing something and time would be bought. When the report is received, the government might take months formulating its response to the recommendations, and may find itself supplied with new reasons why nothing of importance could or should be done. The appointment of the Royal Commission on the Constitution, as a direct response to growing Nationalist feeling in Scotland and Wales, could be viewed in that way. Fourthly, public concern about alleged infringements of the law or the improper use or the inappropriate ambit of state power might produce calls for independent inquiries which a government finds inexpedient to resist. Thus the Privy Councillors' inquiry into the interception of communications in 1957, several investigations into the legal response to terrorism in Northern Ireland, and the Franks Committee on section 2 of the Official Secrets Act 1911 could be said to be instances of such a process.[9] Fifthly, technical issues may arise on which Ministers need expert advice before deciding how to proceed: examples might include the Wilson Committee on Public Records,[10] the several inquiries into the permissible scope of civil servants' political activities, and, indeed, into the civil service itself. Most Speaker's Conferences fit into such a category, too. Lastly, the government itself might decide that a particular constitutional development is timely and commit itself to the principle of reform, and then seek cross-party support for detailed changes. The most notable instances of that would be the Labour Government's commitment in 1968 to reform the composition and powers of the House of Lords, proceeding through the forum of all-party talks, and the present Government's Joint Consultative Cabinet Committee with the Liberal Democrats.

If the government decides, for any of those reasons, to seek outside help, the method to be used more or less chooses itself. If a given topic has a high political content which would be best consid-

---

[9] See respectively Cmnd. 283 (1957); Cmnd. 5185 (1972); Cmnd. 5879 (1975); Cmnd. 7497 (1979); Cmnd. 5104 (1972).

[10] Cmnd. 8204 (1981).

ered by the Prime Minister, or a senior Minister, and their counter-parts, Privy Councillor or inter-party talks would be appropriate. Alternatively, if the situation demands a detailed and independent investigation, representatives of the great and the good may be asked to man a departmental committee of inquiry or a Royal Commission. If a technical aspect of electoral law or procedure falls to be consid-ered, a Speaker's Conference might be set up.

If such an analysis is broadly correct, one general conclusion is starkly clear. Generally governments are reactive, not proactive, in deciding whether to set in motion machinery outside the four walls of government to give advice about constitutional reform. The instances cited in the first five categories just summarized account for practically all of the occasions this century on which Ministers have gone outside government on constitutional matters. Those cat-egories comprise situations in which the government reacted to events which had, in effect, left them with little alternative but to set up some form of consultation or inquiry. It is only in the sixth cat-egory that it can be said that a government decided entirely of its own volition to initiate change and to ease its enactment through external consultations—and then only two actual examples fit at all happily into it. Governments are pushed into activating such mech-anisms in constitutional affairs. They do not look ahead and use departmental committees, Royal Commissions, inter-party talks and the like in a planned way, in order to see how ministerial initiatives on the constitution might be improved. Rather, those mechanisms are resorted to only when events leave them no other choice. Governments much prefer to announce constitutional changes, more or less in their final form, without any prior public consultation or independent consideration of them.

The British constitution represents the triumph of gradualism. It has been shaped by people who have had to work the constitutional system, change often being made as a response to events. The con-stitution has been adapted thus over the years with little reference to constitutional theory. If the constitution is working well enough from a government's point of view, there is no need to change it, even less to set in hand inquiries into the desirability of any of the reforms which are mooted by others from time to time. If a particular problem arises which cannot be ignored, then an appropriate investigation can be mounted and, if necessary, corrective legislation can be passed. If a select committee of either House makes recommendations on a constitutional matter, they will be considered by Ministers, and a response will be made even if no further ministerial action follows. If the government itself perceives that a change in law or practice is desirable, action can be taken. In the light of all that, ad hockery may be seen as not such a pejorative term after all.

This approach, it could be argued, has dealt adequately with constitutional problems in the past. Why change that which works? To those who assert that this system has not adequately answered demands for radical changes the reply may be made that the solution is in the proponents' hands. For they must convince the electorate that they should be given power so that their ideas might be put into practice; or, if that is impossible, they must convince one of the two main parties to adopt them. After all, that latter strategy has recently been effective in relation to the Labour Party, for who would have thought even a short while ago that Labour would commit itself to devolution throughout Great Britain, to the incorporation of the European Convention on Human Rights, to a two-stage plan for the reform of the House of Lords, to a referendum on the electoral system, and so on?[11] Moreover, from the point of view of either a Conservative or Labour government, there would be dangers in moving away from the present manner of going about constitutional reform. If an independent and respected inquiry were to be charged with a systematic review of the constitution, it might recommend solutions which were politically inconvenient for Ministers but resistance to which might be difficult to justify.

In a state of affairs such as this, how might a case for changing the machinery of constitutional reform be expressed? A fundamental point is that the condition of the constitution is qualitatively different in character from any other area of public policy and, as a result, it should not be left entirely to the wishes of the government of the day. British parliamentary democracy implies, at least in theory, that the Government proposes, the Opposition opposes, and

[11] See Ch. 3.

Parliament disposes. In that way national policies are adopted and enacted. But the constitutional rules through which that democracy operates are of transcendent importance. So, for example, the rules by which governments are chosen and through which their policies are put into effect are of a higher order than any other piece of non-constitutional policy which governments seek to carry out once in office. Ideally, therefore, the methods of settling those rules and practices should as far as possible be arrived at through a political consensus rather than through ordinary policy-making and legislative processes.

The earlier examination of the reasons why governments have been moved to set up inquiries revealed a major weakness in the present process of constitutional change, namely, its reactive nature. In the daily grind of parliamentary and political life there seems to be no advantage in devoting time and energy to rethinking aspects of the constitution, at least not unless work had been done on it in opposition (as was the case with the present Labour Government). The tradition is to do nothing, unless the government is forced into action, or wishes itself to implement some particular change. Too little thought is given in government in a planned, unhurried way to whether any part of the constitution could be made to work more efficiently, and how change to one part would affect other parts. It is difficult to think of any other area of national life which has been so effectively cloistered from official scrutiny.

Even when a government does decide that it must do something (or must give the impression of doing something) about a constitutional problem, the existing methods of information-gathering and analysis are not ideal. A mechanism has to be established afresh for each new inquiry: there is no body of continuing expertise which could be tapped, no corpus of technical knowledge which might have been built up over the years and which would be available. There are significant limitations in the terms of reference and the working methods of some of the traditional types of inquiry. A Speaker's Conference, for example, will be concerned only with the details of electoral law and practice, never nowadays with fundamental electoral questions. A Commons departmental select committee can investigate only the department which it oversees, and no government department has sole charge of constitutional issues. Opportunities for public participation can prove to be limited: some inquiries deliberate in public; departmental committees usually invite public contributions, but not always; none has issued draft proposals for comment before finally deciding on recommendations. If public confidence in the constitution and the means of reviewing it is to be enhanced, greater public involvement than is currently allowed would have to become the norm.

Attention has been focused so far on what governments do (and do not do) in relation to the processes of constitutional change. In general governments have steered clear of systematic review of the British constitution. True to that tradition, the late Conservative Government had nothing to do with the unofficial Scottish Constitutional Convention which drew up detailed plans for a Scottish Parliament. The significance of that Convention will be considered in the next chapter.[12] For the moment the lesson to draw from the Convention is that representatives of several political parties in opposition (though in this case not all of them[13]) *can* meet together in order to develop major constitutional reforms, consulting the people who would be most affected by the outcome—and that those parties can reach agreement.

## A Constitutional Commission

The question of how a constitution may be improved is one which is common to all developed states. The technical answer about how formal amendments may be made is invariably provided in the text of a constitution,[14] but that does not necessarily describe any nonlegal steps which should be taken before that stage is reached—whether, for example, public opinion, or political parties outside the government, should be consulted. It is instructive to describe the processes through which the Australian constitution has been reviewed and developed in recent years.[15]

---

[12] See Ch. 3.    [13] The Scottish National Party boycotted the Convention.

[14] For the texts of five national constitutions see S. E. Finer, V. Bogdanor, and B. Rudden, *Comparing Constitutions* (Oxford: Clarendon Press, 1995).

[15] See, e.g. C. Sampford, ' "Recognize and Declare": An Australian Experiment in Codifying Conventions', *Oxford Journal of Legal Studies* 7 (1987) 369. Useful comparative

In important respects Australia's constitution is based on that of the United Kingdom, albeit with a federal structure copied to some extent from the United States. Australia has a parliamentary and Cabinet system of government, and, while she has a written constitution, constitutional conventions have been just as important as in Britain. The Commonwealth of Australia Constitution Act 1900 provides in section 128 that any proposed law which would amend the constitution must be passed by both Houses of the Commonwealth Parliament and be approved by the electors in each State before it may receive the royal assent. Of fifty-four proposals for constitutional amendments made under section 128 since 1901, only a small minority have enjoyed the bipartisan support which in practice is necessary in order to achieve enactment. But what of the pre-amendment stage? Australia resorted to ad hoc investigations into possible constitutional reform, of which the most important were a Royal Commission which reported in 1929, and a Joint Parliamentary Committee which sat from 1956 to 1959. But that ad hoc approach was discarded in two recent initiatives, namely the Constitutional Convention, which deliberated from 1973 to 1985, and the Constitutional Commission, which was appointed in 1985 and reported three years later. The purpose of the Constitutional Convention was to provide a forum of delegates from Commonwealth and State Governments and Oppositions—a gathering of politicians—in which the bipartisan support essential for the success of constitutional amendments might be built. That is not, however, how the work of the Convention developed: its main and lasting achievement was to identify and declare conventions of the Australian constitution and in doing so to reduce many of them to writing. This change of course was largely brought about by the impossibility of achieving cross-party agreement in the wake of the dismissal of the Whitlam Government in 1975. Thirty-three conventions were recognized and declared by the Convention in 1983, including those relating to the powers of the Queen of Australia, the appointment and powers of the Governor-General, the composition

commentary on reviews of the Irish and German constitutions is given in J. Morison, 'The Report of the Constitution Review Group in the Republic of Ireland', and G. Gornig and S. Reckewerth, 'The Revision of the German Basic Law', [1977] *Public Law* 55 and 137.

and functions of the Executive Council, the timing of elections, and the independence of the judiciary. Inevitably, perhaps, some of the statements of conventions seem more helpful than others, but the consensus achieved was impressive, with only a small number of the thirty-three conventions being adopted by votes cast on party lines.

Now while constitutional conventions are important in the Australian (and British) constitutions, and while the work of the Convention put Australia in a better position than Britain by providing what may be described as authoritative texts of the leading conventions, the Convention failed in its original purpose. Accordingly, the Commonwealth Government subsequently announced the setting up of the Australian Constitutional Commission. Its sweeping terms of reference were to inquire into, and in 1988 to report on, the revision of the Australian constitution, in order that it would (*a*) adequately reflect Australia's status as an independent nation and a federal parliamentary democracy; (*b*) provide the most suitable framework for the economic, social, and political development of Australia; (*c*) recognize an appropriate division of responsibilities between the Commonwealth, the States, the Territories, and local government; and (*d*) ensure that democratic rights were guaranteed. The Commission was required to seek the views of the public, business, trade unions, financial institutions, and other interested groups and individuals, and was to hold public hearings for the purpose. The Commission circulated draft proposals widely for comment. Its six members were the Chairman, Sir Maurice Byers, QC (a former Commonwealth Solicitor-General), two politicians, a judge of the Federal Court of Australia, and two academics. In its fundamental review the Commission was helped by five advisory committees, each of which consisted of prominent Australians (including judicial, political, and academic figures), each under the chairmanship of an eminent lawyer or former or serving judge. The committees were directed to involve the public in their work, so that their proposals might be as generally acceptable as possible.

The Constitutional Commission's recommendations were, with some minor reservations, unanimous—itself a major achievement. The Commissioners tried to preserve the framework and principles of the 1900 Act, but they found 'some significant problems' which their recommendations were designed to remove. The report is a massive, two-volume, 1,195-page analysis in which the summary of recommendations alone runs to thirty-two pages.[16] Some recommendations can be mentioned by way of example to show how the Australian process of constitutional review has resulted in radical suggestions for change which seem to have a substantial degree of support. In parliamentary matters, the principle of 'one vote, one value' would be enshrined in the constitution, the maximum term of the House of Representatives would be extended from three to four years, and the Senate's power to reject supply Bills would be altered to a power to delay them for up to thirty days. As far as the executive is concerned, important changes were suggested which would incorporate principles into the text of the Australian constitution which already operate in the United Kingdom constitution—in particular, that most of the powers of the Governor-General would be stated to be exercisable only on ministerial advice. Complaints about the judiciary would be investigated by an advisory Judicial Tribunal, which would establish facts and report to Parliament. And an entirely new chapter was recommended for the constitution—a Bill of Rights for Australia. The Constitutional Commission hoped that its report would contribute to an informed, continuing debate on constitutional issues and would provide the foundation for further proposed alterations to be put to referendums in the future. The fact that the membership of the Australian Constitutional Commission—unlike that of the Constitutional Convention—was not dominated by politicians may have brought it significant public respect. That the clutch of the Commission's proposals which was submitted to a national referendum was subsequently rejected is perplexing, but that only detracts in part from the merits of the whole exercise. Systematic and wide consultation of public opinion, including the publication of draft proposals for comment, provided a model of how policies relating to a constitution should be formulated. But the very wide terms of reference which the Commission enjoyed would not find favour with the Conservative or Labour Parties for any equivalent machinery in Britain.

[16] *Final Report of the Constitutional Commission* (Australian Government Printing Service, 1988).

In the light of the defects in the existing methods of reviewing the British constitution, and of the Australian experience, I want to suggest a new way of doing things to the United Kingdom constitution.

What is needed, I believe, is a permanent advisory Constitutional Commission with the status of a standing Royal Commission. In essence, it might have two tasks. One would be to consider and report on any constitutional provisions which, in its opinion, were in need of clarification or reformulation. For ease of reference, that might be labelled its declaratory role. The other task—its reforming role—would be to consider any aspect of the United Kingdom constitution referred to by a Minister, and to report on whether and how it might be reformed. It must be stressed from the start that the government would have a large degree of control over the Commission's work through the requirement that the Commission could only exercise its reforming function following a ministerial reference. If the Commission were able to gain the confidence of the government, however, Ministers might feel encouraged to increase the number and scope of such references. If (as would be essential) such a Constitutional Commission were to have the support at least of the Conservative and Labour Parties, they would have to have a say in its composition. Discussions through the usual channels might produce agreement on membership. Politicians are among the principal actors in the constitution: it would be essential that the Commission had some politician members and perhaps senior back-benchers in the House of Commons would form the nucleus of the Commission. Equally, the Commission ought to include representatives of the law, industry, universities, and other walks of life. The chairman would have to be a respected and impartial public figure; all the Commissioners would have part-time appointments. The Commission should have access to official advice from government departments, and could seek other evidence; it would need adequate resources, certainly enough to enable it to pay for research. Public consultation, as exemplified by the Australian Constitutional Commission, would be very important, and it would be a welcome development if the Australian example of publishing draft proposals for comment were to be followed. Progress through expert committees, as in the Australian Constitutional Commission, would be an efficient way forward, especially because any other method of working would demand too great a commitment from part-time Commissioners. The Commission's final reports could be laid before Parliament and published as White Papers.

The declaratory role of the Constitutional Commission should not be too threatening to the main political parties, for it would be limited to consideration of existing rules and practices which are unclear or which would be better for being expressed authoritatively: constitutional conventions would be the obvious and main area of work. Parts of the British constitution remain unclear, and disagreement exists between the political parties (and others) about some of its requirements. Examples include the appropriate chain of events which should occur after the return of a hung Parliament; the nature and extent of the Sovereign's powers to dissolve Parliament, to dismiss a government, and to refuse assent to legislation; and the requirements of some aspects of the doctrine of ministerial responsibility to Parliament. The Commission might represent the best hope of giving practical expression to the requirements of what I have called constitutional propriety. Progress might be made by agreeing on and giving definition to the shadowy parts of the constitution which the Commission thought to be both important and yet unclear. If such formulations were not possible, the Commission could suggest what the relevant practice might be for the future. That work would echo the progress made in Australia by the Constitutional Convention. The Constitutional Commission's final reports ought to receive considerable respect from, among others, those who daily work the constitution. Indeed, the Sovereign might choose to follow any relevant Commission statements in the future exercise of her prerogative in difficult circumstances. Were she to do so it would be hard for anyone to accuse her of acting 'unconstitutionally', or of having failed to discharge her duty to act. In that way, reports issued as part of the Commission's declaratory role in times of political tranquillity could prove of value in times of constitutional crisis.

If the Commission proved its worth in its declaratory work, and in carrying out any references which the government might ask it to undertake in the place of ad hoc inquiries, rather bolder references might follow. One such—undoubtedly the most difficult—could be the constitutional problems of Northern Ireland. And one day the political parties might feel able to agree on references concerning fundamental constitutional reform for the United Kingdom, such as, for example, the appropriate powers and composition of the second chamber, or whether any aspects of the royal prerogative might be reduced to statute and perhaps circumscribed. In a forum such as a Constitutional Commission protagonists and antagonists could argue their cases rationally, without the party-political rhetoric which frequently clouds such matters—deliberations worthy of the subjects might take place. Aspects of administrative law, too, might be appropriate for references to the Commission. Other work for it will be suggested in later chapters.

A Constitutional Commission of this type would be a typically British answer to a very British problem. It would be non-statutory, all-party, and advisory. But beyond that it would be a single body which could act as a clearing-house for constitutional ideas, and, being permanent, it should establish a body of expertise which no succession of ad hoc mechanisms could possibly rival. Public opinion would be canvassed to an unprecedented extent. The creation of a Constitutional Commission would put in place a means of taking a planned look at the constitutional system. Naturally, such a Commission would be seen by the Conservative Party as a challenge to its Panglossian view of the main features of the constitution. And any government which set up a Constitutional Commission would certainly want to proceed with caution. But perhaps the two main parties would be wise to give at least private consideration to the idea, because support for it (or something like it) might be the price demanded one day by a smaller party (or parties) for coalition, or a party pact, in the event of the return of a hung Parliament. It should be remembered that Mr Edward Heath as Prime Minister and Leader of the Conservative Party felt able to offer the Liberal Party a Speaker's Conference on proportional representation in February 1974 as part of his suggested coalition deal. Advance planning for a repeat of such an event might be prudent. And, indeed, a Commission along those lines would build on the current constitutional cooperation between Labour and the Liberal Democrats.[17] Whatever

[17] See Ch. 3.

might be the ultimate reason for the establishment of a Constitutional Commission, it might be used in the early days primarily as a replacement for the constitutional inquiries previously conducted by ad hoc bodies, and in furthering its declaratory role. The government which established such a Commission could take some reassurance from the fact that politicians would account for a significant part of its membership, and that *Ministers* would be in command of its reforming function. But the main political parties will have reservations about and raise objections to the principle of such a Commission; two of these objections need to be addressed now.

One (which would certainly be endorsed by the Treasury) is that a Constitutional Commission would require additional human and financial resources, not least to pay for research: by contrast, the existing system is cheap. There are two points to be made about that. A minor consideration is that the cost of the Commission would not be wholly additional public expenditure. Far fewer ad hoc constitutional inquiries would be needed, and the savings on them could, at least notionally, be set against the costs of the Commission. The much more important point is that the shaping of the best structure for the country's constitution is vital, and has as legitimate a claim on public spending as anything else. Why should the country's constitution, of all aspects of national life, be conducted on the cheap? All other areas of law can be calmly considered by authoritative and impartial bodies to ensure sensible development. Most aspects of English law have a Rolls-Royce service from the Law Commission, but the constitution usually has to falter before the government is reluctantly persuaded to despatch the equivalent of the Automobile Association to patch it up. This is completely unsatisfactory. Another objection from the two main political parties might be that the existence of such a Constitutional Commission would slow down the implementation of constitutional changes which they might wish to introduce. This can be explained through the following hypothesis. Suppose that such a Commission had been in existence when the Labour Party came to power in 1997. It might have considered itself bound to refer its clutch of constitutional policies to the Commission for its consideration. There would then have been a delay of many months before the Commission could report on them, and the

Labour Government might not have been prepared to countenance such a delay. Now while things could happen in that fashion, there would be another way of proceeding. References made by the Government to the Constitutional Commission would often be preceded by discussions through the usual channels; Labour, in opposition, could have asked the Government to refer the principal constitutional issues raised in its policy review to the Commission. It might become an accepted practice that, the Commission's other commitments permitting, Opposition requests for references would be acquiesced in by the Government of the day—without, of course, any implication that the Government agreed in any way with the proposals so referred. After consideration, the Commission might approve some of those ideas and reject others. But its role would be *advisory*, and nothing would stop any party putting whatever it wished into its general election manifesto, or prevent it, once it became the government, from implementing its policies whether or not they had been reviewed by the Commission and regardless of any view expressed on them by the Commission.

There would be a separate matter for a Constitutional Commission to consider, which could be important in a strategy for constitutional reform. Parliament is the supreme legislative body in the United Kingdom: the electorate has no formal or legal part to play in the process of enacting legislation. The only power which voters possess is that of changing the composition of the House of Commons at a general election. There is no tradition of formal consultation of the voters about legislation by the government, other than on a dissolution of Parliament. Instead, Members of Parliament are returned to represent their constituents and are expected to get on with that task. There are two difficulties inherent in such a theory of representation which are relevant here. One manifests itself when each major political party has Members of Parliament who have different views on a given issue, so that the electorate's opinion on that issue cannot be taken by means of a general election. For that reason, the view of the electorate about whether the United Kingdom should join the European Community could not have been ascertained at a general election. In any case, an appeal to the electors faces the near impossibility of conducting a general election on one issue. Voters will—irritatingly for the political parties, who might think that they had posed one clear question—inevitably take other factors into account. Then who can say what answer voters had given to the main question? The 1910 general elections were conducted, in the main, on the issue of the House of Lords; the February 1974 poll took place against the background at least of the question, 'Who governs Britain?'; but those were wholly exceptional cases. The other difficulty with this theory of representation surfaces when there is a clear majority in the country on a particular issue, but an equally clear majority of the House of Commons in the opposite direction. Capital punishment is the paradigm case.

The obvious mechanism which could be used to resolve such difficulties is the referendum.[18] When a referendum is proposed, however, Members of Parliament often invoke the shade of Edmund Burke. Are not Members of Parliament, they ask, representatives of their constituents? Must they not decide questions in the House of Commons as best they can, of course taking into account their constituents' opinions as one factor (but only one factor) in making up their minds how to speak and vote? If referendums became the norm, would not Members be reduced to voting according to instructions—and then where would their independence be? (It would be impertinent to remark that Members vote now according to the instructions of their Whips, but let that pass.) Even so, governments and Parliaments have been prepared to embrace the use of referendums in constitutional affairs since 1973, both where the political parties were split internally (as with the European Community referendum in 1975), and where there was a very important issue to be decided (as with the Northern Ireland border polls, and the devolution referendums in 1979 and in 1997). Those referendums were, of course, advisory only: they did not commit the government in any formal sense to act on the results, nor could they have bound Parliament to do so. Is there not a case, based on those precedents, for further constitutional questions being submitted to advisory referendums? Referendums are widely used around the

[18] See generally V. Bogdanor, *The People and the Party System* (Cambridge: Cambridge University Press, 1981); Electoral Reform Society and the Constitution Unit, *Report of the Commission on the Conduct of Referendums* (1996).

world. In Australia and Ireland, for example, they are a compulsory prerequisite for constitutional change; Switzerland uses them as a routine part of the machinery of government; some states in the United States regularly employ the referendum as a means of testing the opinions of electors. Voters in the United Kingdom, as elsewhere, are much better educated than they were in Burke's day, and on the whole they are able to decide issues as intelligently as their elected representatives. Concern would be expressed, no doubt mainly by Members of Parliament, that such an initiative would open the floodgates to referendums on all kinds of other matters. It would have to be emphasised, in trying to assuage such concern, that referendums would be restricted to questions about the British constitution, wholly in line with the historical precedents. Questions relating to the fundamental structure of the constitution are of a higher order of importance than those in other areas of national policy, and that in itself is a reason for resorting to unusual methods to resolve them: no argument arises for employing the referendum in any other policy field.

The Liberal Democrats have always accepted the case for the general use of referendums to provide essential popular authority for major constitutional changes.[19] The Labour Government, too, has recognized the need to obtain the electorate's explicit consent for several (although not all) of its constitutional plans. The Government has already instituted referendums in Scotland and Wales on the Scottish Parliament and the Welsh Assembly; referendums have also been promised on the electoral system for the House of Commons, on possible English regional assemblies, on a new London authority and on a mayor for London, and on whether the Euro should replace the pound sterling. (But Labour intends no referendums on, for example, a Bill of Rights or on reform of the House of Lords.) Even the Conservative Party sees a place for a couple of referendums, one on the outcome of the current Northern Ireland peace process, and another on the adoption of the Euro. That neither main party accepted the usefulness of referendums when this book was first published but now both do is naturally a matter of satisfaction.

[19] See *Here We Stand: Proposals for Modernizing Britain's Democracy*, Liberal Democrat Federal White Paper No. 6 (London, 1993).

## A Noble Enterprise?

Constitutional reform has been the Cinderella of public policy-making in the United Kingdom. It has been generally ignored by the main political parties when preparing their election manifestos—although strikingly not in 1997. Governments have only reluctantly embarked on reviews of constitutional matters, and then have relied on a variety of ad hoc investigations which have been unable to bring any accumulated expertise to bear. Throughout the long history of the British constitution there has been no systematic and authoritative reconsideration of it. Even those who press for radical change seem to have given no thought to appropriate methodology. The degree of public participation in the making of constitutional rules is depressingly low, and yet the formulation of those rules—deciding how the country should be governed—should be a noble enterprise in which citizens have a right to take an important part.

Accordingly, the Constitutional Commission which is proposed would draw on the Australian experience, adopting features which would be of advantage and adapting it so as to reassure nervous politicians. There is much useful work to be done. Where the constitution is unclear, it might bring clarity. When a constitutional problem arises, it could provide analysis and advice. As political confidence in the Commission grew, it might consider the great constitutional issues of the day. The Constitutional Commission could be a means through which the British constitution might be brought out of the last century, where much of it still lies, to meet the challenges of the twenty-first.

# 3 Labour and the Constitution

THE Labour Government which swept to power on May Day 1997 did so committed to make many and vital reforms to the British constitution. Its first Queen's Speech confirmed that Parliament would be asked in the 1997–8 session to approve several changes, including devolution to Scotland and Wales, and the incorporation into domestic law of the European Convention on Human Rights. But even as recently as the early 1980s the Labour Party was still maintaining its historical stance as a constitutionally conservative party, albeit with some notable exceptions (such as a wish to do something about the House of Lords). Given that Labour will be in charge of the constitution for the next few years, an explanation of how the party changed its mind, and an indication of its main constitutional reform policies, may be helpful. Further mention of those policies will also be made in appropriate later chapters.

## New Policies for Old Labour

During the last Conservative Government (especially under Margaret Thatcher) elective dictatorship was revealed at its most awesome. That Government was able to implement its radical policies free, in the main, from significant constitutional checks and balances. It was in that context that the Labour Party—appalled by the substance of Thatcherite policies—undertook a root-and-branch review of all its policies during the 1980s. If it had no other reason to do this, then its defeat at Mrs Thatcher's hands in three consecutive general elections would have provided an irresistible motive. That review came to its conclusion in 1989 when the party adopted a comprehensive statement of policy entitled *Meet the Challenge: Make the Change*.[1]

[1] (London: Labour Party, 1989).

It was during that review process that the Labour Party abandoned its cautious approach to constitutional reform. With the exception of the false starts in trying to devolve power to Scotland and Wales in the 1970s, and of almost reforming the House of Lords in the 1960s, Labour had been almost as constitutionally conservative as the Conservative Party. Indeed, it could be said that down to the 1980s (and with a few significant exceptions) there was almost, in effect, a bipartisan approach to constitutional policy. But what eighty years of political experience had failed to persuade Labour to do ten years of Thatcherism brought about—Labour's conversion to the view that something had to be done about the constitution. The 1989 policy statement committed Labour to the challenging aims of putting individual rights back to the centre of the stage, of providing a major extension of those rights, and of extending democracy. But Labour was not then prepared to overcome its historical antipathy towards a Bill of Rights: the party still thought that because such a Bill would give the judges too much power it had no place in the plans of a party of the left; and in any case Labour believed that such a Bill could not be entrenched, so that its usefulness in preventing a determined Government from further infringing liberty was undermined. Instead Labour decided that, in government, it would sponsor a series of new statutes (on, for example, freedom of information and data protection), statutes which would have been known collectively as a Charter of Rights. Those statutes would have been protected against amendment or repeal by a new elected second chamber: it would have been able to delay any Bill to amend or repeal the Charter of Rights until the end of a Parliament, so that the people could judge the proposal at a general election. Espousal of such a new House of Parliament represented an end to Labour's brief flirtation with unicameralism, for at the 1983 general election it had advocated the total abolition of the second chamber. The party indicated in the 1989 paper that such a new chamber probably would be elected by proportional representation, although it would have only limited powers. But no change was envisaged to the electoral system for the House of Commons: first past the post would stay. Devolution, however, was maintained as official policy, with a commitment to establish a Scottish Assembly or Parliament which would enjoy legislative powers including the ability to vary tax rates in Scotland. Devolution to Wales was mentioned in the policy paper far more tentatively: a Labour Government would carry out wide consultations; local government structures might be altered; an elected body might take over Welsh Office functions. That circumspect approach was, of course, adopted in the light of the decisive rejection of devolution by the Welsh electorate in the 1979 referendum. On Northern Ireland, the party thought that the long-term goal should be a united Ireland achieved by consensual and peaceful means, although (understandably) no details of how that might be brought about were given in the paper; Labour would try, however, to set up a devolved, power-sharing body in Belfast. England would have been given about ten regional authorities to which power would be devolved from Westminster. The administration of justice would have undergone major changes, especially through the creation of a Ministry of Legal Administration to replace the Lord Chancellor's Department, and to take over all of the Lord Chancellor's functions save the purely judicial one of sitting as a judge; the new Minister would have been an MP, not a peer. A judicial appointments commission would have been set up to recommend judicial appointments to the Minister, thus taking the main responsibility for such important and sensitive matters away from politicians.

*Meet the Challenge: Make the Change* represented the fullest commitment ever to constitutional reform by either of the two main British political parties. Labour had positioned itself on the ground which is traditionally occupied by the third party in British politics, but with the obvious practical difference that the Labour Party would be able, one day, to pass them into law. This was, therefore, a self-denying ordinance of great potential practical consequence, because it would reduce the power of central government. With the accession to power in 1990 of an apparently less confrontational and less ideologically driven Prime Minister it would have been understandable if the momentum had gone out of Labour's push for constitutional change. But far from that happening Labour's constitutional plans survived the party's metamorphosis into new Labour during the 1990s, and moreover some of those policies (contrary to what was to be the new Labour trend) were to be given a more radical edge. Labour in the 1990s was, for instance, to embrace for the first time the need to incorporate the European Convention on Human Rights into English law, and was to offer a referendum on voting reform. The party could claim that, however much other old Labour (and voter-unfriendly) policies were abandoned or trimmed in the 1990s, its constitutional reform programme emerged, on the whole, unscathed[2] and, indeed, in some respects in a more challenging prospectus.

Stunned by its fourth drubbing at the polls in 1992, the Labour Party produced a revised statement of its constitutional policy under the title *A New Agenda for Democracy*,[3] which was approved by the annual conference in 1993. That paper concentrated on a number of key areas, in particular, a Bill of Rights, Lords reform, devolution and local and regional government, reform of the judiciary, and freedom of information.[4] Given that the Plant Commission was in the process of conducting a detailed review of the voting system for the Commons, there was no mention of that subject in the paper;[5] after the Plant Report was published Mr John Smith was to commit Labour to hold a referendum on the subject, a promise repeated in his turn by Mr Tony Blair. Of most significance in *A New Agenda for Democracy* was a new and full-hearted acceptance of the need for a Bill of Rights: out went the timid Charter of Rights, and in came a proposal to incorporate the European Convention on Human Rights into domestic law. This would be followed by work on a home-grown Bill of Rights to modernize the 40-year-old European Convention, which would embrace such matters as freedom of information, data protection, and the rights of disabled people. Of more immediate impact than that longer-term aspiration was a decision contained in *A New Agenda for Democracy* on the future of the House of Lords. Now there was to be a two-stage plan, the first being the exclusion of hereditary peers from the House, followed in the second stage by the setting up of a democratically elected second

[2] But the idea of replacing the Lord Chancellor's Department with a Ministry of Legal Administration went the way of other old Labour policies.

[3] (London: Labour Party, 1993).

[4] Some other matters were mentioned briefly, including the need to reform prerogative powers (especially as they are used in foreign affairs and defence).

[5] See Ch. 4.

chamber. The party's commitments to devolve power to Scotland, to Wales (now with a clear promise to introduce a Welsh Assembly), to Northern Ireland, and to the English regions were all confirmed, along with promises to enact legislation on freedom of information, and on the reform of the judiciary. Tucked away at the end of *A New Agenda for Democracy* was another, and surprising, development. Neither the Conservatives nor Labour had up to then accepted that there might be a case for the introduction of a written constitution for the United Kingdom. But the 1993 paper concluded by saying that, while Labour's constitutional reforms would not of themselves amount to a formal written constitution, they would represent, once enacted, a significant step in that direction; and the paper explicitly left open the question of whether at a later stage progress should be made towards formal codification.[6] While that scarcely amounted to a ringing endorsement of a move which would overturn the cen- turies-old basis of the British constitution, it was nonetheless an interesting shift of position.

## Some Influences on New Labour

Constitutional reform policies are not formulated by the political parties in ignorance of work being done by others to reshape the con- stitution. While the Labour Party was developing such policies a number of organizations were formulating proposals for change, aimed in large measure at restraining the power of central govern- ment.[7] Charter 88, the Institute for Public Policy Research, Liberty, and the Democratic Audit (to take just four examples) had all been working on aspects of constitutional reform.[8] Two important newcomers entered the deliberative process in the 1990s, each bring-

[6] That account was a very simplified version of what would be necessary, for it ignored all the other areas which would have to be addressed by a written constitution but which Labour's reforms would not touch. See also D. Oliver, *Government in the United Kingdom* (Milton Keynes: Open University Press, 1991), ch. 11.

[7] See D. Oliver, 'Constitutional Reform Moves Up the Agenda' [1995] *Public Law* 193.

[8] The Institute for Public Policy Research had embraced the whole field of reform by publishing *The Constitution of the United Kingdom* in 1991, subsequently republished as *A Written Constitution for the United Kingdom* (London: Mansell, 1993). This set out the text of a comprehensive (and reformed) British constitution.

ing a distinctive perspective to the debate on constitutional reform. The independent and non-partisan (though centre-left-leaning) Constitution Unit started a two-year programme of work in 1995, geared not to the assessment of the merits or otherwise of particular constitutional reforms, but to an examination of the nuts and bolts of *how* such changes could and should be implemented.[9] Although the Labour Party had written an ambitious shopping-list of reforms for the constitution during the late 1980s and the early 1990s, it had given little or no thought to the question of how the various measures could be enacted, or how each one would relate to the others. Nor had Labour described its legislative priorities for constitutional Bills; and it had given no indication of the speed with which existing parliamentary procedures would permit an ambitious programme to be carried (even less, whether that programme could be achieved along with proper, detailed parliamentary examination of the relevant Bills); nor had the party explained what kinds of public consultation would be necessary or desirable.[10] It was to fill such lacunae that the Constitution Unit was set up. It produced a series of excellent reports, including in particular one which analysed in detail questions of methodology.[11] Those who are concerned with the reform of the British constitution owe a debt to the Constitution Unit for setting out so clearly the practical considerations which must attach to constitutional reform but which are usually, albeit understandably, lost in the arguments about particular institutional reforms.

The Constitution Unit was established after the Scottish Constitutional Convention had been at work for six years. The significance of that Convention[12] lies not only in the detailed and comprehensive work which it carried out on devolution policy but also in my view in its very existence. For the Convention represented the first attempt ever in the United Kingdom to develop constitutional

---

[9] The Unit's terms of reference included instructions to examine the steps necessary to produce a coherent and acceptable programme of constitutional reform, with particular reference to timing and sequence, the parliamentary and consultative processes to be followed, resource implications, and the constraints on any legislative timetable.

[10] Save for commitments to a number of referendums.

[11] *Delivering Constitutional Reform* (London, 1996).

[12] See J. McFadden, 'The Scottish Constitutional Convention' [1995] *Public Law* 215.

policy through debate in a cross-party, and non-party, group. In doing so the Convention sought to draw in different political parties, and representatives of industry, commerce, the trade unions, the churches, and others, so as to raise the level of the discussion above mere party-political exchange. The boycott of the Convention by the Conservative and Scottish National Parties limited its all-party potential, but representatives of the Labour and Liberal Democrat Parties did take a full part in the task of establishing how a Scottish Parliament could work. There are no exact precedents for such an approach.[13] The Convention worked towards as broad an agreement as possible in Scotland and the United Kingdom as a whole on a plan for a Scottish Parliament, and eventually published a detailed final report which, despite the Convention's disparate membership, was a unanimous one.[14] This highly unusual mechanism showed that cross-party (albeit not all-party) agreement on constitutional matters can be achieved.

In 1996 there was to be a development which was more important nationally than the Scottish Constitutional Convention, and which was to continue that important cross-party approach to constitutional reform.

### The Labour–Liberal Democrat Constitutional Programme

Labour's embrace of constitutional reform in the 1980s and 1990s moved it nearer to the Liberal Democrats. True to their radical origins the Liberal Democrats had maintained an unwavering commitment to massive constitutional reform, with the aspiration of crowning it all by the creation of a federal United Kingdom governed through a written constitution which would be adopted by the people at a referendum.[15] Given that Labour and the Liberal Democrats by the early 1990s had separately adopted a largely com-

---

[13] See Ch. 2.

[14] See *Scotland's Parliament: Scotland's Right* (Edinburgh: Scottish Constitutional Convention, 1995).

[15] *Here We Stand: Proposals for Modernising Britain's Democracy*, Federal White Paper No. 6 (London, 1993); *Make the Difference* (Liberal Democrat general election manifesto) (London, 1997).

mon constitutional agenda (with important differences), a logical—
though unprecedented—step would have been to reach a formal
agreement between them on a constitutional programme. In the
summer of 1996, when the return of a hung Parliament at the forthcoming general election was still a possibility, the leaders of the two
parties agreed on an investigation whether such an accord could be
achieved. The setting-up of the two-party Joint Consultative
Committee on Constitutional Reform was the result. Its conclusions
were of crucial importance because they were to form the basis of a
new Labour Government's constitutional policies.

The Joint Consultative Committee's terms of reference required
it to consider each party's then current constitutional reform
proposals, to examine whether there might be enough common
ground to enable the two parties to reach agreement on a legislative
programme on such reform, to consider the means by which such a
programme might best be implemented, and to report. The committee consisted of parliamentary representatives of each party,
together with others sympathetic to the two parties, including a
Queen's Counsel and a Professor of Constitutional Law. The committee took nearly six months to complete its work, and then published a unanimous report (the 'Joint Report').[16] It agreed on a
number of points of principle, points of a kind that are sometimes to
be found in the preambles to state constitutions. Thus the committee noted that the British constitution should secure a government
that is democratic and a society that is open and free; that those in
power should be accountable to the collective wishes and interests of
the people; and that each citizen should have equal rights and
responsibilities in a society where the aim is to guarantee civil liberty, social cohesion, and economic opportunity. The committee
thought that those goals were not entirely secured in the United
Kingdom, especially because power was over-centralized, because
government held more information than ever before with no right in
the public to share it, because Parliament was held in lower esteem
than ever before, and because one House of Parliament was still
composed largely on the hereditary principle. While the Joint Report

---

[16] *Report of the Joint Consultative Committee on Constitutional Reform* (London: Labour
Party and the Liberal Democrats, 1997).

did not indicate legislative priorities to resolve those defects, the Labour leadership subsequently made it clear that legislation for devolution to Scotland and Wales would be given priority by a Labour Government over all other constitutional legislation in the programme.

The Joint Report confirmed the Labour and Liberal Democrat belief that the United Kingdom is one of the most centralized countries in Europe. It noted that demands for greater decentralization had grown in the constituent parts of the United Kingdom, and especially in Scotland and Wales. The two parties accordingly proposed to meet those demands and at the same time (as they insisted) to strengthen the union of the whole kingdom by creating—within the first session of the new Parliament—a Scottish Parliament and a Welsh Assembly. The Scottish Parliament would assume legislative competence over all those matters which are currently the responsibility of the Scottish Office, including health, housing, education, local government, and law and order. The Parliament would be elected by the additional member system. Resources would be found annually for Scotland by the Westminster Parliament, but the Scottish Parliament might have the power to vary the basic rate of income tax by three pence in the pound upwards or downwards. A Labour Government would hold a pre-legislative referendum in Scotland on the basis of proposals to be published in a White Paper. Two questions would be posed in that referendum, one asking for support for the general scheme, the other for the tax-varying plan. If there were a positive vote at the referendum legislation would follow, and clearly parliamentary opposition to it would be harder to sustain in the light of a positive referendum vote in Scotland. As far as Wales was concerned, the Joint Committee committed a new Government to establish an Assembly elected by the additional member system (at the urging of the Liberal Democrats, acquiesced in by the Welsh Labour Party). It would take over Welsh Office functions, control quangos, and provide a forum for the development of policy. It would have no powers to enact primary legislation or to raise revenue. This would be a much more modest affair than the Scottish counterpart. A referendum would be held in Wales on the basis of a White Paper. The Joint Report made no reference to

Northern Ireland; it did make some modest suggestions for regional assemblies in England.[17]

The Joint Report recalled that a debate about the appropriate system for electing MPs to Westminster has gone on throughout the twentieth century, and said that the question ought now to be concluded by the people. The Labour Party, however, has no policy on whether the voting system should be changed, although Tony Blair is personally not persuaded of the desirability of change (while some of his senior colleagues, like Robin Cook, are committed to proportional representation). On the other hand the Liberal Democrats, like the Liberal Party before them, are wedded to proportional representation (PR), one obvious reason being that their hopes of translating their share of the vote at parliamentary elections more closely into seats won could only come about under PR. Despite that difference of view between the two parties, they agreed in the Joint Report to advocate the additional member system for the new assemblies in Scotland and Wales, and they also agreed that a national referendum should be held on the voting system for the House of Commons early in the new Parliament. A commission would be set up to agree which PR system should be placed before the voters in the referendum as the only alternative to first-past-the-post: voters would be allowed to vote only for the status quo or for the specified alternative: all other PR—and indeed all other—systems[18] would be left out of account. The justification for this stance—not articulated in the Joint Report—was that the proponents of the various PR systems might split the pro-PR vote if they were given a multi-choice question, with the result that the vote for retaining first-past-the-post might exceed that for any single PR system. The commission would have to report within a year, and legislation would then be passed to enable the referendum to be held. It was (and remains) unclear what recommendation, if any, a Labour Government would make to the electorate in the referendum, or whether there would be an

---

[17] Indirectly elected regional chambers would be set up first, followed (where there was local demand) by referendums on directly elected assemblies. The assemblies would bring some democratic accountability to the existing Government Offices for the regions, and to many quangos.

[18] Such as the alternative vote, and the second-ballot system: see further Ch. 4.

agreement to differ for Ministers who could not support any recommendation. This proposal can be criticized on the ground that it
would deny a choice to proponents of other systems, such as the
alternative vote and the second-ballot system, as well as to the proponents of other PR systems. A multi-choice referendum ballot
paper would accurately reflect the electorate's wishes, but that consequence is to be sacrificed so as to maximize the pro-PR vote.[19]

Despite the dispiriting auguries of failed attempts to reform the
House of Lords, Labour and the Liberal Democrats agreed in the
Joint Report that the hereditary principle is indefensible as the basis
for providing a large part of a House of Parliament, and accepted the
need for legislation to be passed to remove hereditary peers from the
House of Lords. The Joint Report acknowledged that some hereditary peers, including some of the cross-benchers, who have contributed to the work of the House should receive life peerages to
enable them to remain members: the cross-benchers, according to
the Joint Report, should continue to account for about one-fifth of
the composition of the House after the hereditaries had been
excluded. Labour and the Liberal Democrats agreed that, following
the removal of the hereditaries, no one party should enjoy a majority in the House of Lords; they also proposed that, over the course
of the new Parliament, the party balance of the remaining life peers
should be altered through new creations more accurately to reflect
the proportion of votes obtained by each party at the general election. All that would constitute the first stage of Lords reform. In the
second, a joint committee of both Houses would consider the structure and functions of a new second chamber which was both democratic and representative. No reference was made in the Joint Report
to any referendum being held on that scheme, although it would be
very likely that a further general election would have occurred before
plans for an elected second chamber could be implemented. How
long this second stage would take, how likely it might be that a cross-
party agreement on a new chamber could be achieved, and whether
the final solution would prove acceptable to the House of Commons
was and still is unclear.[20]

[19] See further Ch. 4.    [20] See further Ch. 5.

When the United Kingdom took a major part in drafting the European Convention on Human Rights after the Second World War it was assumed that the resulting international treaty would be incorporated into English law. As with most international treaties it could not become part of English law unless a statute were passed for that purpose. The Convention was ratified by the United Kingdom in 1951, but incorporation has still not taken place, despite attempts over the years by backbench MPs and peers to do so: no Government before 1997 had accepted the undesirability of the status quo, even though under the current law British citizens who wish to enforce their rights under the Convention have first to exhaust their remedies in English law in British courts and then, if they are still not satisfied, go to Strasbourg to seek redress from the machinery of the Convention. That is a lengthy process, taking as much as seven years in some cases. The Liberal Democrats have long advocated the drafting and adoption of a new British Bill of Rights, and would pause first before doing so only to incorporate the European Convention. Historically the Labour Party had not accepted either proposal, very largely as a result of its distrust of the judiciary whom it has seen as reactionary and hostile to left-wing principles. But the Labour Party changed its mind on this issue in the early 1990s, partly because it believed that the judiciary had tried to safeguard individual rights during the long period of the Conservative Government, partly because Labour no longer thought that Parliament alone could be relied on to be the main guarantor of liberty, and partly because the Labour Party itself had moved from the left to the centre ground. The Labour Party now accepts—and repeated its view in the Joint Report—that legislation should be introduced to incorporate the European Convention into English law. The Labour–Liberal Democrat Joint Report acknowledged that the sovereignty of the British Parliament would not be affected by this step—in other words, no attempt would be made to entrench the Convention against easy amendment or repeal. It is widely (though not universally) thought that it would be impossible in the British constitutional system to effect such entrenchment.[21] Rather

---

[21] See further Ch. 8.

than attempt to do so, therefore, the two parties proposed that Ministers should be required to make clear to Parliament whether any provision of a subsequent Bill was, or appeared to be, inconsistent with the Convention. If it was, then Parliament could judge whether to accept the Bill. The two parties would also set up a new joint select committee of both Houses, and a Human Rights Commission, which would monitor the working of the incorporation Act and help individuals to get redress under it. The Joint Report was vague about whether a new, home-grown Bill of Rights would be introduced. It did state that the Convention would need to be updated over time as a model for modern constitutional protection of human rights. In any event incorporation is wholeheartedly to be welcomed: it should cut out the delay, expense, and inconvenience of going to Strasbourg, and does not rule out the adoption of a new and modernized Bill of Rights one day.[22]

Greater freedom of information was also envisaged in the joint Labour–Liberal Democrat agreement. The parties believe (as they put it in their document) that open and accountable government and freedom of information are essential to democracy, but that the workings of government are currently hidden behind a veil of secrecy. In order to correct that situation a Freedom of Information Act would be introduced to give the public access to information about the workings of government and to allow individuals to see information held about them by government agencies. There would be statutory exemptions, including the power to withhold information on grounds of national security, or the need to protect personal privacy, or to keep confidential policy advice given to Ministers by civil servants. The scheme would be policed through independent machinery. The overall aim, according to the Joint Report, would be to shift the balance decisively in favour of the presumption that official information should be made available publicly unless there were a justifiable reason not to do so.[23]

Two general observations may be made about the parties' overall joint constitutional programme. First, whatever the merits and demerits of each of the proposals, at least they emerged from more

---

[22] See further Ch. 8.
[23] The Government was to publish a Bill in 1998.

than merely the internal policy processes of one political party: the joint agreement on these proposals shows that constitutional reform in the United Kingdom can be advanced across the party-political divide. But the joint committee's work involved no public involvement in the policy-making process. Admittedly, the joint committee was set up within six months of the latest date by which a general election had to take place, and most of that time was needed to hammer out agreement. But ideally constitutional reform should be brought about through wide public debate and the involvement of as many political parties as possible, because the constitution of any country is the concern of all its citizens, all of whom should be able if they wish to take part, however indirectly, in its development. The state of a national constitution is of a higher order of importance than any other area of public policy. It is profoundly to be hoped that the Labour–Liberal Democrat cooperation, and indeed the precedent of the Scottish Constitutional Convention, will mark the first steps towards the creation of a more inclusive, more permanent, and wider-ranging public review process dedicated to constitutional reform in the United Kingdom. Secondly, the Joint Report would admit the electorate into the reform process through a national referendum on the voting system, and through local referendums on Scottish, Welsh, and English devolution. Apart from those opportunities for citizens to have a direct say, their approval for the rest of the constitutional package has been taken as implicit in the election of the Labour Government at the general election in 1997 in which other issues were always bound to predominate. There was, for example, no plan in the Joint Report to consult the people explicitly on the issue of reform of the House of Lords. Nor would any special legislative procedures or parliamentary majorities be required to implement the proposed changes, processes which would constitute an attempt to mark out constitutional legislation being something special and apart from other law-making. Indeed, the committee published nothing on that part of its terms of reference which required it to consider the means by which a reform programme might best be implemented.[24] All of that is a matter for regret.

[24] On referendums generally, see Ch. 2.

## New Labour in Power

What, then, is likely to be the shape of the British constitution after one (or even two) terms of the Labour Government? Labour's huge 179-seat majority at the 1997 general election gave the party the constitutional authority to seek the enactment of its programme, based on its manifesto.[25] The manifesto pledges on constitutional reform generally followed *A New Agenda for Democracy* and the Joint Report. Thus there were commitments on Lords reform, a Freedom of Information Act, devolution to Scotland, Wales, and the English regions, incorporation of the European Convention on Human Rights, and the continuation of the Conservative Government's peacemaking process in Northern Ireland. No mention was made, however, of setting up a judicial appointments commission,[26] or of any review of prerogative powers (both of which had been trailed in *A New Agenda for Democracy*). The first Queen's Speech contained legislative proposals for the eighteen-month-long 1997–8 session, and showed the new Government's constitutional priorities for its first parliamentary session. Legislation would provide for referendums in Scotland and Wales on the Government's devolution plans, followed if approved by substantive devolution legislation. There was to be a Bill to incorporate into United Kingdom law the European Convention on Human Rights. A Bill would provide for a referendum on a directly elected strategic authority for London and a directly elected London mayor. The Government would consider how the funding of the political parties should be reformed. In Northern Ireland, the Government would continue to seek reconciliation and a political settlement. And a White Paper would be published detailing plans for a Freedom of Information Bill.

To demonstrate its commitment to devolution, the Labour Government introduced the Referendums (Scotland and Wales) Bill into the House of Commons as its very first Bill. Under the resulting Act the people of Scotland and Wales were able to vote at

---

[25] *New Labour: Because Britain Deserves Better* (London: Labour Party, 1997).

[26] But the Lord Chancellor's Department was to issue a consultation paper in the summer of 1997, but this was postponed indefinitely. See Ch. 9.

referendums on the Government's proposals for a Scottish Parliament and for a Welsh Assembly. White Papers giving details of the plans were published on which the electorates could make up their minds.[27] The votes were held in September 1997. Scotland gave a resounding endorsement for a Parliament with tax-varying powers (74 per cent voting for the Parliament, 63 per cent for the tax powers, on a 60 per cent turnout). The Welsh were much more equivocal, voting 50.3 per cent to 49.7 per cent in favour of a Welsh Assembly on a turnout of 51.3 per cent. The substantive devolution Bills have now been introduced into Parliament.

In view of its Queen's Speech commitments to constitutional change in Scotland and Wales, to incorporate the European Convention, and to design freedom of information legislation, the Cabinet decided that it could not legislate on House of Lords reform in the 1997–8 session (even though that session would last six months longer than usual).[28] But it kept its options open for such legislation to be introduced in the following session, and in deciding on its timing the Government would no doubt take account of peers' treatment of Labour's current legislation, especially on devolution. Ministers were keen to point out that Lords reform was in the Government's programme, but denied (not very convincingly) that they were wielding Lords reform as a sword of Damocles over peers' heads.

The new Prime Minister allocated responsibility for the constitutional reform programme to the relevant departmental Ministers, that programme being overseen by a Cabinet committee chaired by him, and subsequently by the Lord Chancellor. Much more radically he announced the creation of a standing Joint Consultative Cabinet Committee, again chaired by him, on which Liberal Democrat parliamentarians would have five seats.[29] The main purpose of the Committee is to take forward the two parties' joint constitutional programme, but other matters of common concern are not ruled out from discussion. This carrying over from opposition to government

[27] *Scotland's Parliament*, Cm. 3658 (1997); *A Voice for Wales*, Cm. 3718 (1997).

[28] Moreover, a Bill to exclude the hereditaries would be technically simple: see, e.g. Constitution Unit, *Reform of the House of Lords* (London, 1996), app. A.

[29] See 299 HC Debs. *113* (written answers 29 July 1997).

of bipartisan cooperation is to be applauded. It is an initiative which possesses some of the important qualities indicated in the previous chapter which should be enjoyed by the machinery of British constitutional reform.

Cynical observers will dismiss Labour's transition from conservatism in constitutional affairs to being a party which champions major alterations to the British constitution as a political reaction to Thatcherism and four general election defeats. Of course that political reality has played its part, but only a part. The Labour Party had seven years after Margaret Thatcher's demise to trim constitutional policies which would be inconvenient for a Labour Government and to move itself nearer to Conservative attitudes to the constitution. But it did not do so, and to the contrary developed several policies in ways that would make life even more awkward for Labour Ministers. And Labour did all this despite the political adage that there are no votes in constitutional reform. There is no sign that, now Labour is in government, it intends to do other than give effect to its plans to transform whole areas of the British constitution.

For those who believe that constitutional reform should wherever possible proceed by consensus, or at least by cross-party cooperation, the last few years have been encouraging. Whether through the unofficial and broadly based Scottish Constitutional Convention, or through the two-party Joint Consultative Committee, or through the Joint Consultative Cabinet Committee, the process of constitutional change has been broadened out beyond single-party initiatives. The use of referendums as a means of legitimizing constitutional change is now accepted—although not for every important constitutional development. Organizations such as the Constitution Unit have shown the value of careful and concentrated work on the mechanics of particular constitutional developments. All of that has come about in the last decade or so. There is, however, still reliance in Whitehall on traditional machinery of government methods for delivering constitutional reform: the case for a single senior Minister and perhaps one government department to spearhead change has not yet found favour.

The Labour Government's huge parliamentary majority, a cohesive parliamentary party, and an Opposition that is still adjusting to its ignominious rejection by the electorate all mean that the Government's legislative programme should pass quite easily through the House of Commons. The House of Lords is in a relatively weak position to delay matters, given the Government's clear manifesto authority for its constitutional changes—which included a death sentence for the existing House. By the end of this Parliament, therefore, the British constitution should embrace the European Convention on Human Rights as part of domestic law, a Freedom of Information Act, and a Scottish Parliament and a Welsh Assembly. And if the people at referendums so wish it the British constitution would prescribe that subsequent Westminster Parliaments be elected by PR, and would provide for an all-London council and directly elected mayor. The House of Commons will certainly have revamped its internal procedures; the House of Lords may no longer have seats for hereditary peers. That would all amount to a radically different constitution, and one which a future Conservative Government would find hard to overturn.

# 4 Parliamentary Democracy

THE House of Commons has many functions, but two of them are (or should be) of overriding importance. They are to provide the government with its political legitimacy, and to represent the electorate. The House of Commons fails in both those purposes.

## The Failings of Democracy

The reverence which politicians accord some ancient constitutional notions does not always spring from sentiment. The Queen in Parliament is very much a case in point. Legal sovereignty must reside somewhere in every political system. It is well settled that legal sovereignty in the United Kingdom is located in the Queen in Parliament, and that (to the satisfaction of subscribers to orthodox learning at any rate) there is little which the Queen in Parliament cannot do.[1] In strict law, of course, the Queen in Parliament is the Queen, the Lords, and the Commons coming together to enact legislation. This assembling is notional rather than real, and indeed the whole concept now has about it an air of unreality. For the political power of two component parts of the trinity—the Queen herself and the House of Lords—has been subordinated by convention and by law to the wishes of the House of Commons; in its turn, the House of Commons has permitted its political authority to be exercised by the government; and as a result the Queen in Parliament in effect means the government. Legal sovereignty is in practice exercised by—or at least at the request of—Ministers. Small wonder that

---

[1] Even the Queen of Parliament cannot legislate inconsistently with European Community law: *R* v. *Secretary of State for Transport, ex p. Factortame (No. 2)* [1991] A.C. 603. There are many awkward questions about the omnipotence of the Queen in Parliament which will not be gone into here.

Governments (and Oppositions wishing to be governments) revere the idea of the Queen in Parliament, or parliamentary sovereignty, and can become agitated about threats to sovereignty from, for example, the European Union. Legal sovereignty gives them immense political power, largely unchecked by any other authority.

But what of citizens? On the optimistic assumption that they have tacitly acquiesced in this constitutional development, what do they get in return for allowing Ministers untrammelled legislative power to interfere in their lives? In Diceyan terms, citizens as electors are left with political sovereignty.[2] As long as Ministers, as the effective legal sovereign, allow regular general elections, the electorate retains the power to alter the composition of the House of Commons and so to confirm or reject the government of the day. The political sovereign chooses the government through the indirect method of selecting an electoral college, known more familiarly as the House of Commons. In theory, the college meets to choose a government, and indeed could pick a different government at any time. In practice, the electoral college has achieved its purpose as soon as the results on general-election night give one party at least one-half of the Commons seats plus one. From that moment, the Prime Minister or his successor is endowed with the political authority to take full charge of the nation's affairs, and in due course to implement his party's policies through legislation and otherwise. But this seemingly simple legitimating process conceals difficult questions. The most notorious is, of course, whether it may be said at all convincingly that a government which achieves a majority of seats is legitimate if it obtains only a minority of electors' votes—which has been the result of every general election this century bar four.[3] Politicians from the main parties none the less—and not surprisingly—maintain that the party make-up of the House of Commons is everything: a government which has a majority of Members of Parliament behind it has all the political legitimacy that is required. The Members sitting on the government benches provide the outward and visible sign of that legitimacy. That way of looking at things has, moreover, the approval

---

[2] A. V. Dicey, *Introduction to the Study of the Law of the Constitution*, 10th edn., ed. E. C. S. Wade (London: Macmillan, 1962), 70–6.

[3] Those of 1900, 1918, 1931, and 1935.

of a constitutional convention which holds that the person who leads the majority party in the House of Commons is entitled to be appointed Prime Minister by the Queen. It is simply not done, in the British constitution, to look behind the election returns to check the arithmetic of how those Members were elected.

And so the citizen's exercise of ephemeral political sovereignty is complete on marking a cross on a ballot-paper every four or five years. That is not a very active citizenship, but is rather the consequence of a lopsided bargain to which electors are assumed to have assented and which politicians stoutly defend. This imbalance would not matter so much if the government paid close heed to citizens' wishes. To what extent, however, do the government and the House of Commons take into account voters' views between elections? Put another way, how well does the Commons discharge its representative function?

If anyone should know in what sense Members of Parliament are representative,[4] it is Members themselves. They would almost certainly refer the inquisitive voter to Edmund Burke, perhaps even citing the famous passage from his 1774 *Speech to the Electors of Bristol*: 'Your representative owes you, not his industry only, but his judgement; and he betrays, instead of serving you, if he sacrifices it to your opinion.' That firmly puts the voter in his place: in ruling out any suggestion that constituents might order their Member how to act or vote, a relationship is established in which the Member of Parliament can behave condescendingly to his constituents. For although the citizen may address his opinions to his Member of Parliament on local and national issues, it must be clearly understood that the Member may reject those opinions out of hand. The adoption of Burke's thinking by Members of Parliament down the years is another instance of politicians making good use of old and very agreeable constitutional notions. Naturally, Members of Parliament will say in their defence that they treat their constituents with disdain only at

---

[4] For a concise and very useful historical account of theories of representation, see C. Harlow, 'Power from the People? Representation and Constitutional Theory' in P. McAuslan and John F. McEldowney (eds.), *Law Legitimacy and the Constitution* (London: Sweet & Maxwell, 1985). See also M. Dummett, *Principles of Electoral Reform* (Oxford: Clarendon Press, 1997).

their peril, for the clock starts to tick towards the next polling day as soon as a general election is over. If a Member is dismissive of his constituents' opinions and needs, then they can contemptuously reject him at the next election. But how many Members have actually been unseated by their constituents in such circumstances?[5] Does the theory that unrepresentative Members are penalized by the loss of their seats actually translate into practice? *Governments* are rejected at elections; Oppositions are voted into power; but that is a very different process. Burke's view of the relationship between Members and their electors has itself become grossly misleading. Members of Parliament can certainly form judgements on issues before them free from pressures from their constituents, but another force—that of party—has subverted their independence. This is especially the case in the House of Commons itself, through the whip system, but the power of party in the constituencies is also very strong, particularly in the selection of parliamentary candidates. While Burke's theory freed Members from any threat of being mandated by their constituents, it provided a political vacuum which the political parties have been delighted to fill.

During the life of a Parliament, the Member owes a duty to represent (in whatever fashion is appropriate) all his constituents, rather than just those who voted for him. This must be so, for otherwise millions of voters would enjoy no parliamentary representation at all given that in many constituencies more people vote for losing candidates than vote for the returned Member. (Indeed, in safe seats, many electors regularly vote for parties which have no chance of winning, and for their pains are described as wasting their votes.) That a Member represents all his constituents is a fine and accepted theory, but what does it actually imply as far as accountability is concerned? If a Member fails to represent his constituents properly, or if he misbehaves in a way which incurs their wrath but which (to their minds) produces an inadequate response from the House of Commons itself, they can do nothing to reject him as their Member until the next general election. He might be deselected as his party's

---

[5] Mr Neil Hamilton's loss of his seat to an Independent in the 1997 general election is certainly one example. Mr Hamilton had attracted heavy criticism for improper financial behaviour while an MP.

candidate, but this amounts only to the prospective loss by him of the seat, and in any case is an action dependent on his own party alone. Should Members have a five-year lease with absolutely no risk of earlier foreclosure? And what of those happy holders of indefinite leases, sitting Members in safe seats? There the selection of a Member is settled by the party holding the seat in whatever way seems appropriate to them. This may be by a constituency-party meeting where only those interested enough or able to turn up have a say, or it may be by a postal ballot of party members. The electorate is, in effect, presented with the party's candidate, to like him or lump him. He will not have the support of electors who vote for other parties: he may not (depending on the form of selection procedure) even have the support of most voters in the constituency who are in his party. In what sense does he start his parliamentary career truly representative of his constituents?

It has become fashionable, if not actually obligatory, for those reflecting on the British constitution to damn the first-past-the-post electoral system[6] out of hand. It is identified as a root cause of much that has gone wrong in the United Kingdom, and which, in constitutional matters, has produced unrepresentative Members of Parliament and the growth of party power to the detriment of the individual. Anyone who is not a Conservative or Labour supporter who writes of its merits risks being portrayed in a Bateman-type cartoon with the description, 'The person who spoke well of the British voting system.' Risking such a fate, I want to indicate some of the advantages of that method of voting.

The British voting system is simple. Voters are entirely familiar with the easy task of marking one cross against one name on a ballot paper, and then later that day or the next learning the name of the victorious candidate who secured more votes in the constituency than any other person. There is no question of election officials distributing and redistributing votes according to any mathematical (and possibly complicated) formula. The party that gets a majority

---

[6] Sir William Wade, *Constitutional Fundamentals*, rev. edn. (London: Stevens & Sons, 1989), 9–10, criticizes the use of that term and argues that it is more accurate to speak of a relative majority system. He is quite right, but for the sake of familiarity I will stick with the old phrase.

of Commons seats wins the election. It would be hard to devise a more straightforward method of election involving a secret ballot in 659 constituencies, each having as many candidates as wished to stand. The first-past-the-post system is also decisive. After a general election British voters expect to know the name of the next Prime Minister quickly, and if there is to be a change of government, they expect to see television pictures of furniture vans outside Number 10 Downing Street on the day after the election as a physical sign of the transfer of power which they have brought about. No question arises—at least, not usually—of politicians conducting negotiations to make practical political sense of what the electors have decreed through the ballot boxes. The identity of the next Prime Minister is usually known before voters go to bed on election night. Indeed, with the advent of exit polls, the result is confidently predicted by the broadcasting media moments after the polls close at 10 p.m., even before a single ballot box has been opened. (The predicted government majority has occasionally been gloriously inaccurate, although so far not to the extent of naming the wrong party as the winner.) In that way the first-past-the-post system *is* democratic: it is as a direct result of their ballots that voters produce a parliamentary majority for one party, which then forms the government. There is no post-election fudging of the voters' decision. This simple and decisive process produces stable governments, in the sense of one-party majority administrations. Save for the February 1974 result, every general election since 1931 has produced a parliamentary majority for one party. Given the cohesion of party, such a government is normally assured of being able to conduct its business until the Prime Minister decides to submit himself to the electorate. This helps all those who wish to plan their affairs on the assumption that there will be no change of government, and perhaps even no dramatic change of policy, for the following four or five years.

Implicit in all that is the assumption that general elections are primarily about power, rather than representation. Voters are mainly concerned with conferring political power, rather than achieving an exact correlation between numbers of votes cast for any party and the number of seats which it achieves in the House of Commons. By and large people vote for or against the government. Perhaps more accurately, they vote to keep the Prime Minister in office, or to throw him out. Given a mass television audience, it is most unlikely nowadays that any party would try to win a general election by offering a collective leadership rather than an attractive leader worthy to be Prime Minister. The personalities of the party leaders are vitally important in British general elections, which have become presidential in character, and consequently it may be said that it is important that a general election unambiguously gives power to one prime ministerial candidate. It may be that the price to be paid for that in a first-past-the-post system is that the number of seats won will not precisely match the votes given for all parliamentary candidates. Before a radically different—and no doubt more representative—voting system were adopted, it would be of paramount importance to know whether the goal of fair representation in seats won for votes cast was to be equated with, or made superior to, the goal of clearly conferring power on one party.

A final attribute of the existing system is the rooting of each Member of Parliament in his local soil. While the relationship between a Member and his constituents may sometimes be far from ideal, considerable benefits must flow from it because no one suggests that Members should cease to represent a defined geographical area. Not even the most zealous champions of proportional representation want the perfect proportionality which is secured in, for example, the Netherlands. There, electors vote for names from each party's national list of candidates, and legislators are returned in strict proportion to votes cast for the parties. These legislators represent everyone and no one and everywhere and nowhere. The conscientious British Member of Parliament keeps in touch with his constituents, through surgeries and otherwise, on parochial, national, and world matters, and most people seem to think that this is highly desirable.

Full credit should be given to these advantages before it is decided to sacrifice the current method of voting on the altar of electoral reform. But there are, of course, disagreeable aspects of the first-past-the-post voting system, which in essence are unfairness, and the imbalance in favour of the elective function and against the representative function.

The one-word indictment of the first-past-the-post method is unfairness. It is unfair to smaller parties, unfair to electors who do not vote for the winning candidate, and even unfair to the Conservative and Labour Parties. The first-past-the-post system is ideally suited to a society which is predominantly and accurately represented in its legislature by only two parties, one in and the other out of government: for that reason it exists happily in the United States of America. But it is notorious that the United Kingdom is not such a society. Smaller parties achieve substantial political support, as evidenced through the number of votes cast for them, but they secure derisory numbers of Members of Parliament. So, for example, in the February 1974 general election the Liberals received over six million votes, but only fourteen Members: the Conservative and Labour Parties each polled just under twice that total, but secured respectively 297 and 301 seats. At the October election in the same year, the Liberal vote dropped to some five million, and they lost one Member; the Conservative vote fell by about a million, but they only lost twenty Members; Labour's vote dropped slightly, but the party's representation *increased* to 319 Members. The greatest unfairness to the smaller parties occurred at the 1983 general election, at which the Liberal–SDP Alliance secured over 25 per cent of the electorate's vote—almost eight million crosses—but only 4 per cent (twenty-three) of the seats in the House of Commons. Labour, on the other hand, with some 27 per cent of the vote, was rewarded with 32 per cent (209) of the seats, while the Conservatives won with 42 per cent of the vote and 61 per cent (397) of the seats. At the last general election Labour secured 44 per cent of the votes cast but 63 per cent of the seats; the Conservatives received only 31 per cent of the popular vote and 25 per cent of the seats; the Liberal Democrats obtained 17 per cent of the national vote but only 7 per cent of the seats. A scheme which is capable of producing such results does violence to the concept of fair play as the British understand it. For the Conservative and Labour duopoly to be broken under the present voting system, there would have to be a political convulsion in which one of those two parties was replaced by a third party—as the Liberals were replaced by Labour earlier this century—or a change to proportional representation for elections to the House of Commons.

Unfairness is wrought, too, on those voters who do not vote for winning candidates. This is not a small, disaffected minority that cannot take its defeat: it is usually a *majority* of those who vote at general elections. While those in this losing majority have the satisfaction of exercising their right to vote, the practical reward for doing so is non-existent. Voters who do not support the winning candidate in the 450 or so Commons seats which are safe for one party might just as well stay at home, for all that happens to their votes is that they are merely recorded in election statistics. In those seats, the constituency party chooses—democratically or otherwise—the person who is later ritually affirmed as the local Member at the general election. A voting system which permits millions of voters to ask themselves whether it is worth bothering to vote is subversive of democracy.

Those who reap largess from this electoral system do not deserve much sympathy when it discriminates against them. But the first-past-the-post method does operate unfairly against the Conservative and Labour Parties in parts of the United Kingdom, and the phenomenon of the safe seat is, again, the cause. So, for instance, the Labour Party's parliamentary representation has been virtually eliminated in south-west England; at the 1997 general election the Conservatives' limited representation in Scotland and Wales was reduced to no representation at all. The two main parties in those parts of the country must be as disillusioned as are (say) the Liberal Democrats throughout the United Kingdom.

Inextricably linked in the voting system with unfairness is the supremacy of decisiveness over representativeness. The first-past-the-post system has developed into a mighty engine which can be relied on to produce a government from one of the two principal parties. But in that development the purpose of gathering a House of Commons which is broadly representative of the electorate has rather faded. This would possibly not be as important as it is if the elective function worked on the basis of a majority of voters conferring a parliamentary majority on the winning party. Patently, however, it does not do so. Mr Tony Blair's landslide parliamentary majority of 179 seats in 1997 was achieved with only 44 per cent of the votes cast. Mrs Thatcher's 144-seat landslide majority in 1983, and her huge 102-seat majority in 1987, were achieved even though on both occasions some 57 per cent of votes were given to other parties. Almost 60 per cent of voting citizens voted *against* those governments. This is by no means a recent phenomenon. Attlee's 146-seat majority in 1945 was won on under 48 per cent of the vote, and indeed no winning party has been supported by half or more of those going to the polls since the general election of 1935. Are the virtues of the British electoral system—simplicity, decisiveness, its ability to produce stable governments, and so on—so self-evident as to justify such distortions of the electoral will? Is it really necessary to have a voting system predicated either on the representative function, or (as in Britain) on the elective function?

In all this—and in more than this—the political parties have become over-mighty. President Kennedy began his Inaugural Address by declaring, 'We observe today not a victory of party but a celebration of freedom.' What may be observed in British democracy, by contrast, is indeed the victory of party—over a person's ability to be elected and re-elected to the House of Commons, and over how he conducts himself when he arrives there. To stand a chance of being elected a Member of Parliament, one of the two main parties, or in some places the Liberal Democrats, must enfold the candidate in its colours. It is rare in England for an Independent candidate to be elected, even at a by-election. In Scotland and Wales, Nationalists are often returned; Northern Ireland has its own pattern of politics, although Unionists always make up most of the province's representation. But those differences in Scotland, Wales, and Northern Ireland do not touch the majority of House of Commons seats located in England, where the grip of the main parties is very tight. To be re-elected, the Member must be reselected in his constituency. Clearly, a Member should not be returned to Westminster for life: it should be possible for the party on whose ticket he was returned to remove its imprimatur. Equally clearly, though, this party process of reselection reduces the Member's independence. The Labour Party pioneered the regular reselection process: every Labour Member must undergo reselection in his constituency once in every Parliament, and several Labour Members have thereby indirectly lost their seats when their constituency parties denied them their backing.

The Conservative Party is more circumspect over reselection, but deselection does occasionally happen. In 1990, for example, Sir Anthony Meyer's constituency party deselected him as the Conservative candidate—but then he had, after all, caused an election the previous autumn for the leadership of the Conservative Party by standing against Mrs Thatcher.[7] The Conservative machinery for selection and reselection varies from constituency to constituency but, like Labour, physical presence at the relevant meeting is often required. The Liberal Democrats choose their candidates by secret ballot at constituency party meetings, each member having one vote, and provide easily obtained postal votes for those who will not be there.

The power of party is offensive to democracy if it causes a Member wishing to be confirmed as his party's candidate to defer to his constituency-party activists to such a degree that he represents them rather than his constituents. Indeed, the less democratic the nomination exercise, the more likely it is that the Member will not be accountable even to the broad mass of people belonging to his party in the constituency. The views of supporters of his party who do not wish to be active in such things as selection and reselection may count for very little. If the Member is a realist he will understand that he must accord great respect to those who actually have the ability to reselect him; and yet that important power is wholly unrecognized and unregulated by law.

Once returned to the House of Commons the Member's party expects him to be loyal. This is not entirely unfair or improper, for it is the price of the party's label which secured his election. But the question is whether the balance of a Member's obligations has tilted too far in favour of the requirements of party. The nonsense that a whip—even a three-line whip—is no more than a summons to attend the House, and that, once there, the Member is completely free to speak and vote as he thinks fit, was still being put about, by the

---

[7] Another Conservative Member, Mr John Browne, was also deselected in 1990: his Winchester constituency party did so after the House of Commons had suspended him for twenty sitting days for not registering certain of his interests. After the rejection of Mrs Thatcher as Conservative leader, several Conservative Members who had supported her rivals faced deselection attempts.

Parliamentary Private Secretary to the Prime Minister, as recently as 1986.[8] No one can honestly believe that. Failure to vote with his party on a three-line whip without permission invites a party reaction. This will range (depending on the circumstances and whether the offence is repeated) from a quiet word from a Whip and appeals to future loyalty, to a ticking-off or a formal reprimand (perhaps from the Chief Whip himself), to any one of a number of threats. The armoury of intimidation includes the menaces that the Member will never get ministerial office, or go on overseas trips sponsored by the party, or be nominated by his party for Commons committee memberships, or that he might be deprived of his party's whip in the House, or that he might be reported to his constituency which might wish to consider his behaviour when reselection comes round again. Such threats might seem like blackmail to a member of the public; he might also query how a Member of Parliament could be anything like a free agent in the House in the face of such strictures. Does the Member not enjoy the parliamentary privilege of freedom of speech? How can his speech be free in the face of such party threats? The answer to the inquiring citizen is that the whip system is part of the conventionally established machinery of political organization in the House, and has been ruled not to infringe a Member's parliamentary privileges in any way. The political parties are only too aware of the utility of such a system, and would fight in the last ditch to keep it.

Members of Parliament do, of course, defy the orders of their party from time to time. Supporters of the government do so occasionally even when the consequence will be that the government will lose a division. To do that takes courage. Sometimes Members' consciences will permit them to do no other. Yet the government goes rolling on, annoyed, embarrassed, but still in office, bolstered if necessary by a vote of confidence in the administration.[9] Occasional losses of votes on legislation do not really count for much, in the sense that they do not threaten the government's life and in any case only account for a tiny proportion of the total number of divisions in the House of Commons.

[8] In a letter quoted to the House of Commons: 95 HC Debs. 595 (14 Apr. 1986).

[9] Defeats on votes of confidence are very rare and have related to very special circumstances.

Within their own hands Members of Parliament hold the remedies for many constitutional ills, particularly those which result from the overweening power of party. Professor Ganz has put in this way:

> They have the vote and if they used it more frequently in accordance with their judgement rather than the party whip, the power of the government would be markedly curtailed . . . But it would be simplistic to underestimate the pressures of party loyalty and the party whips. The most potent antidote to the latter would be a system of voting in secret in the House of Commons instead of walking through the division lobbies.[10]

But then, as she points out, no government is going to introduce secret voting in the House of Commons. If less deference to the dictates of party and greater reliance on personal judgement and constituency feeling are desirable—as I am sure they are—Members need some additional reason for greater resistance to the Whips' entreaties. A new mechanism which would help them do so will be suggested a little later.

### Towards a New Democracy

I want to turn now to possible reforms in British parliamentary democracy. Let us start at the beginning with a Member of Parliament's selection as a party candidate. The political parties quite rightly have the power to decide who should stand for election to the Commons in their names. But given that that decision effectively elects the Member in the majority of constituencies, it must be right that the method of selection should receive the close attention of the law to ensure that it is democratic, fair, and properly conducted. The only way to make sure that those attributes were achieved would be to introduce primary elections.[11] The central aim of such elections ought to be that the choice of a party's candidate in any constituency should be broadly representative of party opinion in that constituency. The selection should not be left to a committee or to a particular meeting (both of which contain the danger of choice by

[10] G. Ganz, *Understanding Public Law*, 2nd edn. (London: Fontana Press, 1994), 27.
[11] This is not a new idea: see e.g. Wade, *Constitutional Fundamentals*, 23–4.

faction), or to a body in which any section of the party (such as trade unions) has a disproportionate say in the outcome. There is no substitute for a secret ballot conducted by post in which every registered and paid-up member of the constituency party has an equal vote.[12] Without such an election a parliamentary candidature should be void. Postal votes are now widely available for parliamentary elections; the inadequacies of meetings where votes are taken about trade union matters have been recognized and countered by legislation providing for postal ballots.[13] The whole drift of democratic development has been towards votes being cast secretly and by methods which ensure that everyone has the opportunity to vote.

Primary elections to choose parliamentary candidates are not unknown in the British political parties. The Liberal Democrats require that they be used; Labour has a selection procedure; some Conservative constituency associations conduct postal ballots of their members. The parties should not, therefore, be taken aback when it is suggested that such commendable procedures should be made universal and fully democratic. The casting of votes on polling-day does not amount to the real choice of Member in many constituencies: therefore, the candidate-selection process through which the choice of Member is really made ought to receive the same recognition in the Representation of the People Acts as the parliamentary balloting process itself. The law should open its eyes to candidate selection so as to control it in the public interest. Reselection, too, should be general, regular, and democratic. Putting candidates through primary elections would be an exercise of limited value if the lucky winners in safe seats were then rewarded with leases for life. So a fresh primary election would be required in each constituency once in every Parliament if anyone wished to challenge the existing candidate.

As with most suggestions for change, practical considerations will no doubt be cited as reasons for holding back. None seems weighty. Each constituency party would have to maintain adequate registers of members, but that is scarcely an impossibly onerous task in these days of computer-lists of names and addresses held at national party

---

[12] I will not go into the question of what method of voting would be appropriate.

[13] The Labour Government has acknowledged the soundness of that legislation and will not seek its repeal.

headquarters. The cost of primary elections might not be insignificant, and certainly the question of how public money might be provided would be a proper consideration.[14] Exemptions from the requirement of primary elections would need to be made, for example, for candidates who wished to stand independently of party, or who were representatives of small, or non-national, parties. Candidates such as the ubiquitous Lord Sutch, or those standing for, say, the Green Party, should accordingly not be required to undergo primary elections supervised by law.

In my view, however, democratic primaries and reselections are not enough, for too much power would still reside in the hands of the political parties. People who were not supporters of the Member's party would obviously have no say in the primaries, and even those who were registered party members would only be able to call the Member to account at a fixed time in each Parliament. This would not cover the case in which a Member of Parliament was seriously unrepresentative of general constituency opinion, or whose personal behaviour fell below standards acceptable to his constituents. What is needed is some additional device to ensure that a Member pays heed to constituents' views (rather than just to party opinion) and which gives him an alternative defence against the blandishments of the Whips. Rousseau believed that the grant of sovereignty by the people to the sovereign power was conditional and could be recalled by the people at any time.[15] It is the notion of recall that is attractive, not in the sense of the people as a body taking back the powers of government and legislature, but as a recognition of the conditionality of the trust which electors in each constituency put in their Member of Parliament. Constituents should be given a recall power so that if a given proportion of voters in a constituency wanted to force their Member to fight a by-election, they could vote to do so, and if the necessary vote were achieved, his seat would be vacated. The recall ballot would be conducted by the Returning Officer and enshrined in statute. Naturally, there would have to be a high threshold to activate the recall, so that frivolous or spiteful

---

[14] The cost of trade union postal ballots is met by the government.

[15] See J.-J. Rousseau, *Social Contract*, ed. G. D. H. Cole (London: Dent, 1973), introduction, p. xxvii.

attempts to unseat a Member would be frustrated—a simple majority of those voting in the recall ballot would not be sufficient. That threshold would need to be arrived at through a combination of a prescribed minimum turnout and a prescribed minimum vote in favour of recall.

What sort of conduct might attract the operation of the recall power? First, a Member might have misused his membership of the House, for example to further his personal financial interests in a manner offensive to his constituents. They might consider that the action taken against him by the House (or, indeed, lack of action) was inadequate. If the Member were also a Minister when his conduct was called into question in his constituency, then the Prime Minister's reaction might upset sufficient of his constituents that the recall power was activated. Even if the Minister resigned his office, his constituents might take the view that his seat should be forfeited as well. On the other hand, the Member's personal life ought not to be a proper subject for inquiry through the recall power, unless it affected his ability to function effectively as a Member of Parliament. Secondly, a Member might not represent the opinions of his constituents on some important local or national issue, for example on local matters on which the Member failed adequately to reflect constituency feeling, perhaps because he put his loyalty to the government line, or his cooperation with the Whips, above his duty to represent his electors' views. Environmental questions could be especially in point: the routing of major new roads or railway lines, the siting of power-stations or other unwelcome buildings, and the like, might all cause a clash between departmental or commercial wishes and the happiness of constituents, and it would, perhaps, be no bad thing if a Member were to place his constituents' happiness above other claims on him. Issues of national policy, too, can divide Member from voter, but it would be important to argue that issues of private conscience, such as abortion or capital punishment, should be exempt from the threat of recall as they are exempt from the discipline of the Whips. Thirdly, the use of a recall power might be particularly apt when a Member changed his party but declined to resign his seat and fight an immediate by-election. It is not unreasonable to expect a Member who crosses the floor of the House, or who joins a new party, to resubmit himself quickly to the electors who had returned him in different colours.[16] Of course, in all those three areas of controversial conduct the ordinary processes of reselection might well result in the Member being dropped as his party's candidate (and obviously would definitely have that result in the third case). But that could only occur when the time for reselection came; and in any event the constituency would still have the Member representing them until the next general election. A cleaner and more timely parting of the ways would be preferable. Sometimes a suspended sentence does not meet the case.

Good constituency Members of Parliament would have little to fear either from primaries or from recall. The recall power might be little used, or at least might be little used successfully, but it would serve its purpose by existing as a permanent reminder that those who have entrusted a person to represent them in the House of Commons do not place that trust unconditionally. A major advantage of a recall power would be the blow which it would strike against the élitist and patronizing view taken by some Members that their constituents should elect them every four years or so and then should largely leave them alone. A recall power would give greater practical meaning to the notions of representation and accountability—or at any rate would provide a practical consequence for misrepresentation. It would also act as a counterbalance to the drag of the Whips. Floating the idea of a recall power is not, however, an attempt to push the balance between obligations to party and obligations to constituents too far in favour of the latter, so that Members became mere automatons dancing to the touch of their electors. To prevent that from happening, the precise rules governing the recall power would have to be such as to reserve its bite only for those cases where a large body of constituents believed, on clear criteria, that a by-election was demanded.

There are several other questions about a recall power which would have to be answered. Would recall votes be cast solely on party lines? Of course they might be, especially in safe seats. But

---

[16] Those Members who joined the Social Democratic Party in 1981 did not fight by-elections; nor did the three Conservative Members who crossed the floor during the 1992 Parliament.

even if this did happen, would that be a bad thing? Even *without* a recall power the constituency party would retain a (democratized) selection and reselection process, and it could choose another candidate for the general election if it so wished. The recall power would speed up that process so as to bring about a more timely change of representation. In less safe seats, the threshold necessary for recall to be activated ought to mean that one party's view about the sitting Member would not of itself be enough to trigger a by-election. How, then, would a recall power mesh with a Member's parliamentary privilege of freedom of speech and action? The answer to that may be achieved through another question: how does the whip system truly and fairly mesh with parliamentary privilege? The honest answer is that it does not, and to the extent that a recall power would cause the Member to take care to conduct his affairs acceptably and to respond to constituency opinion, it would further diminish a Member's theoretical independence. But would voters be bothered to turn out to vote at what might be two further constituency polls— the recall vote and any resulting by-election?[17] This questioning of whether it is worthwhile establishing further formal opportunities for people to express their wishes because they might not use them is sometimes the last refuge of the anti-democrat. 'All these elections!', many politicians will cry. Governments in particular aver that people do not like being called frequently to polling stations, and that they will become bored by democracy if they are asked to participate in it too much. What is nearer the mark is that governments fear elections. So much is at risk in them—political power, the trappings of office, and keeping opponents where they belong. I believe that participatory democracy requires more elections, not just the current rate of general elections plus a few random by-elections supported by candidate-selection procedures which occasionally produce unrepresentative candidates. The right to elect and to reject representatives is—or should be—fundamental, and citizens should have proper and adequate opportunities to do so.

Radical reformers will dismiss the idea of more elections—whether primary, selection, or recall—as the equivalent of applying sticking-

---

[17] Actually three if the selection ballot is counted as well.

plaster to a comatose patient, or will use some equally dismissive phrase. For they will say that it is not the number but the method of elections which needs drastic change. So let me now grasp the nettle of electoral reform. Anyone doing so ought to keep at the front of his mind the facts that the Conservative Party is entirely opposed to voting reform, that many Labour Party supporters are wedded to first-past-the-post (and that the Labour Government is committed only to hold a referendum on electoral reform),[18] and that only the Liberal Democrats enthuse about it. Persuading either—and certainly persuading both—of the two main parties to support radical changes to the voting system would be difficult, and perhaps impossible.

Desirable features of the existing first-past-the-post system include simplicity, decisiveness, political stability, a recognition that general elections are as much about conferring power as achieving accurate representation, and the rooting of Members of Parliament in constituencies. Unattractive features of the system are unfairness, and the imbalance which has arisen in favour of the function of choosing a government and away from representation. Quite understandably, for many people the only way to remove those disagreeable aspects is by applying the patent medicine of proportional representation.[19] The only point on which the purveyors of this remedy are all agreed is the negative one that there must be no resort to the national party-list method, as operated in the Netherlands. In that system there is one national constituency in which seats are allocated to the parties in strict proportion to the national votes achieved by the parties. Not only would such a system remove British Members' constituency bases, but it would also give representation to a political party in the House of Commons on a mere 0.15 per cent of the national vote.[20] Rather, proportional representationalists in the United Kingdom talk up, according to taste, either the regional-list system, or the single

[18] See Ch. 3.

[19] For a comprehensive review of voting systems see the *Report of the Working Party on Electoral Systems* (the Plant Report) (London: Labour Party 1993).

[20] See D. Butler, 'Electoral Reform', in J. Jowell and D. Oliver (eds.), *The Changing Constitution*, 3rd edn. (Oxford: Clarendon Press, 1994), 388. This could, of course, be avoided by requiring a party to obtain a minimum threshold before it was awarded any seats, as is the case, for example, in Germany.

transferable vote, or the additional-member system.[21] A brief reminder of how they work may be helpful.

The *regional-list method* allows voters in given areas to vote for the candidate of their choice from his party's approved list of candidates. The votes cast in favour of each of the party lists are then totalled and distributed proportionately to each party. The order in which individual candidates on each list are voted for is used to decide how many of those candidates are elected. A variant of this system is used in Finland, for example, and was used for elections to the Northern Ireland Forum elected in 1996. The system is now to be used for elections to the European Parliament (in place of first-past-the-post). A disadvantage of that sort of scheme is the loss of the single-Member constituency.

The *single transferable vote* method requires large constituencies, usually of about five Members, in which voters rank candidates in order of preference. A quota is arrived at in each constituency at each election by dividing the total number of votes cast by the number of Members to be elected plus one. As soon as a candidate obtains that quota in first preference votes he is elected; any votes of his over that quota are then allocated to the second preferences expressed. If places then still remain to be filled, the candidates with the fewest votes are eliminated in turn and the second or subsequent preferences are reallocated until all vacant places are filled. The single transferable vote method is used in Ireland and for the Australian Senate. There is British experience of it in Northern Ireland, for local government and European Parliament elections, and in elections to the Northern Ireland Assembly in 1973, 1975, and 1982. Its use for elections to the House of Commons and to a new elected second chamber is currently urged by the Liberal Democrats. The drawbacks of the system include the complicated counting which is involved (how many electors would really understand and have faith in it?), and the necessity of having very large constituencies each of some 300,000 voters.[22]

The *additional-member system*, used in Germany and advocated for Britain by the Hansard Society Commission in 1976,[23] gives each

---

[21] Ibid. 387–91 for brief descriptions.     [22] Ibid. 389–90 for other problems.
[23] Report of the Hansard Society Commission on Electoral Reform (1976).

elector two votes. One is cast for the candidate of his choice, to represent him in a single-member constituency; the other is cast for the party of his choice. Seats are allocated from the party lists so that, taken together with the representatives elected from the candidates' list, each party has a number of representatives in proportion to the votes cast. There may be (as there is in Germany) a threshold to be achieved before a party obtains any seats in the legislature on the basis of the votes for the party lists. An objection to the additional-member method is that the choice of candidates is removed from the locality and taken by the parties at national level—but representation in proportion to votes cast is achieved, and the advantages of single-member constituencies are retained. The new Scottish Parliament and Welsh Assembly will be elected by this method.

If a method of proportional representation were introduced for elections to the House of Commons, there might as a result be a lurch too far in the direction of the representative function and away from an efficient means of electing a government. It is that possibility which gives some force to the view that proportional representation is undemocratic. Under first-past-the-post, a change of government is normally brought about by the voters at a general election. But in systems which deny an overall majority to any one party—as any proportional method is likely to do—that elective function is removed from the voters and is given to the smaller parties which are represented in the legislature. The German experience of 1982 is often cited, in which the Free Democratic Party changed partners, withdrawing from one coalition government and putting another in its place—all without any reference to the voters. So, too, in the United Kingdom smaller parties, such as (but not only) the Liberal Democrats, would have a similar power under a regime of proportional representation to alter governments between elections, a government-making and government-breaking authority which would be wholly disproportional to the votes accorded them at the general election. Such a situation would be even more objectionable if the smaller parties refused to give any indication before a general election of which of the major parties they would favour. Indeed, the main third party refused to give such an indication before the 1983, 1987, or 1992 elections—although before the 1997 poll the Liberal

Democrats said that they would not support the Conservatives in a hung Parliament. Voters would be denied what is perhaps the main advantage of the present voting method, the selection of a government. In effect, voters would have to delegate that task to elected politicians. In choosing a coalition or minority government, those delegates might have little regard to what voters had indicated about government formation through the pattern of their votes. This is a serious constitutional objection to proportional representation, and in my view would amount to too great a tilt of the electoral scales in favour of the representative function and away from the voters' government-choosing function. One unbalanced set of scales would be replaced by another unbalanced set, whereas the quality which needs to be aimed at is equilibrium, even though it is unlikely to be achieved perfectly.

Some misgivings about proportional representation can, it is true, be exaggerated. For instance, the advantage under first-past-the-post of returning a relatively stable government has also been achieved in Ireland and in Germany, although of course by having coalition governments in office. Even the phenomenon of revolving-door governments in Italy rather conceals the fact that one party has dominated the administration since 1948.[24] Again, the local links which are preserved in single-Member constituencies are not necessarily lost: they are retained under the additional-member system in Germany (for the election of half the representatives). A proliferation of parties in the legislature does not follow inevitably: while it has happened in the Netherlands, Israel, and Italy, the number of parties in the Irish and German legislatures actually went down after the introduction of their current electoral systems. What *would* follow from the introduction of proportional representation in the United Kingdom would be the routine election of a hung House of Commons.

It is, perhaps, unnecessary to dilate on the implications for the British constitution of the demise of single-party majority government, because detailed consideration has already been given to

---

[24] Despite that, in 1993 Italy adopted the first-past-the-post system to fill three-quarters of each parliamentary chamber, leaving the remainder to be returned by the former proportional representation system.

them.[25] Many settled constitutional and political practices would
have to be reassessed and changed. Party manifestos would become
no more than invitations to treat, formally published to the voters
but in fact issued to the other parties for negotiation after the electoral verdict had been given. The formation of a minority or a coalition government, and the question of granting dissolutions of
Parliament, would be matters which could not be entirely settled
without a reconsideration of conventions involving the Queen.[26]
Party discipline in the Commons would become much more lax: governments would have to inform and persuade Members in more than
one party, rather than just relying on the Whips to deliver votes. The
doctrine of ministerial responsibility would have to be modified to
accommodate coalition government. None of this represents an insu-
perable bar to proportional representation, but they are matters
which would require very careful examination before any change was
put into effect. How unattractive, however, all of this would be to
the two main parties when set against the present certainties of elective dictatorship!

And so the tents are pitched in two entrenched camps. In one rest
the immovable supporters of the electoral status quo, while in the
other gather the hardy fighters for proportional representation. One
reason for the stalemate may be that conservatives fear that the only
alternative to the first-past-the-post system is immediate proportional representation, while radicals assume that the only alternative
to whatever type of proportional representation they espouse is the
current intolerable method of electing Members of Parliament. To
change the metaphor, each side seems to want to keep hold of nurse
for fear of finding something worse. Proportional representation
would only come about if the Labour Government's promised
national referendum were to endorse a system of proportional
representation, or if the Conservative Party underwent a truly
remarkable change of heart (involving the throwing away of the regular dose of unrestricted power which the present voting system

[25] See, e.g. V. Bogdanor, *Multiple-Party Politics and the Constitution* (Cambridge:
Cambridge University Press, 1983); R. Brazier, *Constitutional Practice*, 2nd edn. (Oxford:
Clarendon Press, 1994), ch. 3.
[26] See Ch. 7.

brings), or if there were an electoral upset in which a small party obtained sufficient Members so as somehow to squeeze voting reform out of one of the larger parties as the price of vital parliamentary support. It is, of course, possible that the British electorate will opt for radical change at the referendum on the voting system. But is there no option other than either staying where we are or changing to proportional representation? Might there not be a middle way down which the two sides might grudgingly travel? I suggest that there is, and that it would involve either the second-ballot, or the alternative-vote, systems.

The second-ballot system is a very straightforward method of election which is used in France.[27] Voters cast their ballots in single-member constituencies, thus preserving the representative's local links. Any candidate who receives at least half the votes cast in his constituency is elected. If, however, no candidate has such absolute majority support there is a second ballot a week later, which is a run-off between the two candidates who came top of the original poll, together with any other candidate who obtained at least 12½ per cent of the votes in it. Often only the top two candidates qualify for the second ballot, in which case the subsequent winner is bound to receive an absolute majority of those voting in the constituency. The second-ballot system avoids the complicated redistributions which are a feature of any proportional representation method of election. It normally produces one-party government. The second-ballot method is unattractive to proportional representationalists because it maintains the balance in favour of the government-choosing function over the representative function. But if the second ballot were introduced for elections to the House of Commons, the days of the Member of Parliament returned by only a minority of those who voted in his constituency would usually be over, and there would be political upsets in numerous constituencies: no longer would a candidate who might, under the present voting system, expect only 40 per cent of the vote necessarily take the seat. For example, the Conservative candidate might poll 40 per cent of the votes, the Labour candidate 35 per cent, the Liberal Democrat 10 per cent, and

---

[27] It is also used to elect the President of the Republic.

other candidates 15 per cent. Today, the Conservative would win outright—even though 60 per cent of the voters preferred someone else. Under the second-ballot system, the Conservative and Labour candidates would fight it out in the run-off. Voters who had supported the Liberal Democrat might vote Conservative or Labour in the second round, and the seat could go either way. Those electors whose candidate did not survive the first ballot would be able to vote again with all the other voters in the second ballot, and in that sense everyone's vote would count. The delay of a week between voting would allow the parties in each constituency where a Member had not been returned in the first round to consider how to recommend their supporters to vote in the second round. Majority governments would at last often be worthy of that name: their legitimacy would be unquestionable, because it would be based on both a majority of seats in the House of Commons *and* on Members having the support of an absolute majority of voters in most constituencies.[28]

Objectors to the second ballot criticize the need for voters to return to the polls seven days after they have done their civic duty. Such an onerous consequence can be avoided (although the possible political benefits which may accrue in the hiatus will be lost) by opting for the alternative vote. This method, which is used for elections to the Australian House of Representatives, has actually received the approval in principle of the House of Commons in 1918 and in 1931 for its own elections. It avoids the need for a physically separate second ballot by allowing voters to express their successive choices in one voting operation. The aim is to elect representatives by absolute majorities. Voters are asked to say which candidate, again in single-member constituencies, they would support if their first choice did not receive an absolute majority. To do so, they number the candidates on the ballot-paper in order of preference. A candidate who gets at least 50 per cent of the first preference votes is elected. If none does so, the candidates with the least votes are eliminated in turn, and their second preference votes are redistributed, until one candidate has an absolute majority. While this does nothing to bring about national proportionality between votes cast and seats won, it has all

---

[28] For criticism of the alternative-vote and of the second-ballot systems, see E. Lakeman, *How Democracies Vote*, 3rd edn. (London: Faber, 1970), 59–68.

the considerable advantages of the second-ballot method without the inconvenient second visit to the polling-stations, although clearly the redistribution process (which is still much simpler than most proportional methods) would need careful explanation for voters.

If the pressure for electoral reform became irresistible, the second ballot or the alternative vote might provide models which one of the two main political parties might support as a reasonable compromise, moving away from the first-past-the-post but falling well short of proportional representation. They might, at least, provide more defensible redoubts than does the current voting system. Radical reformers will reject the second ballot and the alternative vote and will continue to insist on the purity of proportional representation. But they need to show greater electoral realism: they are not going to get proportional representation overnight from either of the main parties, and it might be better for them, as an interim measure in their terms, to support the second ballot or the alternative vote if either the Conservative or Labour Parties did so as well. Simple, decisive, producing stable parliamentary politics, providing governmental legitimacy, and fairer than the present method—these are qualities of the second ballot and the alternative vote which, in my view, deserve very close assessment.

Whether, and if so how, to reform the British voting system would be questions for which a Constitutional Commission would be tailor-made.[29] In such a gathering—which would include representatives of the political parties—quiet, calm deliberation, while perhaps not disentangling every knot, would at least bring the independent and the committed together. Research, evaluation, public consultation, and debate should all contribute to synthesis. Many issues would need to be addressed by the Commission. What theory (or theories) of representation are appropriate for the British House of Commons? What is the British electoral system designed to achieve? What are the practical advantages of the first-past-the-post system, and of proportional representation systems? What are the drawbacks in those methods, and to what extent might a different model overcome them—without introducing others? How satisfactory is the power of party over the

[29] See Ch. 2.

selection of parliamentary candidates and over Members of Parliament? What value might there be, in an attempt to offset the influence of party, in the refreshing breeze of democratic primary elections, reselections, and recall, all governed by law?

The political parties will not be distressed that I have offered answers to such questions, but they might object that such matters are not the concern of any independent grouping such as a Constitutional Commission. Politicians, after all, are the experts who have to work British democracy; they have an intimate and unrivalled knowledge of its workings and they have to persuade voters to support them. The voting system and connected issues are, in a blunt politician's terms, no one else's business. It is, however, that very interest which politicians have which makes it essential that informed and independent opinion should contribute to the development of parliamentary democracy. To take an analogy, independent Boundary Commissions exist simply because the delimitation of parliamentary constituencies cannot be left entirely to the parties in Parliament (and certainly not the House of Commons alone), because they have a direct and vital interest in the result. It is not suggested for a moment that a Constitutional Commission should *decide* the rules of British parliamentary democracy, but it is proposed that the formulation of those rules should no longer be left entirely within the walls of Westminster. Such a proposition does not seem preposterous. Indeed, the Labour Party has accepted that politicians should not make a decision on their own about the future of the voting system, and the Labour Government is to provide for a national referendum on the issue.

## Coda: Inside the Commons

Changes to House of Commons procedure are a matter for that House alone, normally following a report from the Select Committee on Procedure. The new Labour Government, however, caused a new Select Committee on the Modernization of the House of Commons to be established. Its task is to consider how the practices and procedures of the House should be modernized, and to make recommendations. Further consideration is also being given in government to the funding of political parties, perhaps along the lines proposed by the Houghton Committee in 1976.[30] It is good to see that one of the main political parties recognizes the need for procedural change in the House of Commons. The Liberal Democrats in effect support many of those ideas, and have other suggestions for procedural reforms too.[31]

The House of Commons is as firmly wedded to the two-party system within its walls as the Conservative and Labour Parties are wedded to an electoral system based on the convenience of only two parties.[32] The Commons chamber is built for only two parties, physically opposite each other;[33] the Leader of the Opposition has a status raised way above that of any other opposition party leader; Government and Opposition business managers fix parliamentary business through the usual channels, merely informing the other parties of the result; the Opposition has the lion's share of Opposition days, leaving the third-largest party the privilege of choosing the main debate on only three days of the year. A fairer deal for the smaller parties represented in the House—and for whom millions of electors vote at general elections—is surely needed. Such a deal might involve the smaller parties being formally consulted in the planning of Commons business, being provided with salaries for their party leaders (perhaps qualifying on the basis of votes secured and seats won at the previous election), and more Opposition days being accorded them. While reform of the voting system awaits a change of mind by at least one of the two main parties, the House as a whole must be urged to concede that it ought to take some account in its procedures of votes cast by electors as well as seats obtained by the parties—a principle already accepted by the House in the allocation of 'Short' money to opposition parties to help with the cost of their research. A better deal for backbenchers on both sides of the House

[30] *Report of the Committee on Financial Aid to Political Parties*, Cmnd. 6601 (1976).

[31] See *A Parliament for the People*, Liberal Democrat Policy Paper No. 20 (London, 1996).

[32] What follows is elaborated in R. Brazier, *Constitutional Practice*: 201–3, 230–1.

[33] The first permanent home of the House of Commons was in St Stephen's Chapel, and Members sat in the choir-stalls. That configuration of Members sitting on two sides of the House has been followed ever since.

ought to include some real opportunity to scrutinize government tax, borrowing, and spending policies, given that, as the Public Accounts Committee has reported, 'Parliament's consideration of the annual estimates—the key constitutional control—remains largely a formality'.[34] It would also provide more scope and time for legislative initiatives by private Members, because at present private Members' Bills, to be successful, must either be unopposed or be government Bills in all but name. More time is also needed for debate of departmental select committee reports, so few of which are actually considered by Members on the floor of the House, rather than just receiving an often brief government response in the form of a White Paper. Such changes would deprive the government of some of an invaluable asset, time. While the hours of working of the House could be reconsidered so as to afford some compensation, there may not be much scope for lengthening the daily sitting given the outside careers of many Members and the committee and other work which must be fitted somehow into a parliamentary day. More modest alterations should be looked at, such as, for example, a routine allocation of time to all major public Bills in order both to keep up a reasonable rate of legislation and to save the time now routinely wasted on tedious three-hour guillotine debates.[35] On average, an extra parliamentary day each year would be gained by that change alone. Another possibility would be to lengthen the parliamentary year—although the House of Commons already sits for more days in the year than any other legislature in a large democracy.

While the details of procedural reform must be a matter for agreement between the major parties at least, the simple point which I urge upon them is that the views of people in other parties, and of backbenchers on both sides of the House, ought to count for more in the practices of the House of Commons. If the much larger question could also be addressed of how the electoral system might be made fairer while retaining the strengths of the present method of voting, there might be in prospect a major enhancement of British parliamentary democracy.

[34] 8th Report from the Public Accounts Committee, HC 98 (1986–7), para. 2.
[35] More limited proposals from the Select Committee on Procedure to reform the use of the guillotine did not find favour with the House in the 1985–6 session.

# 5  The Second-Chamber Paradox

RARELY have Government plans for constitutional reform been formed in the agreeable setting of a golf course. But it was on Rye golf-links that the two-writ scheme was put to the Leader of the House of Lords in Mr Harold Wilson's Cabinet, Lord Longford, and where he became convinced of its efficacy.[1] The Cabinet, too, was subsequently taken by it, and in 1968 the Labour Government proposed that there should be two categories of peers, one made up of nominated life peers who could speak and vote, the other (mainly hereditary peers) having only the right to speak and having no right to pass membership on to their successors.[2] Despite such pleasant beginnings and the later gathering of all-party support for the scheme, all crowned by the approval of the House of Lords itself, the Bill to implement this major reform failed to pass the House of Commons.

Failure to make substantial progress on Lords reform has dogged all governments who have grappled with it. There has been no shortage of official analyses of the strengths and shortcomings of the upper House, or of attempts to improve it. The preamble to the Parliament Act 1911 set the scene for the replacement of the House by an elected chamber, but as the preamble lamented, 'such substitution cannot be immediately brought into operation'. That bare statement of intent was clothed with a detailed plan by the Bryce Committee after the First World War.[3] After the Second World War, a number of reform matters were settled in principle between the leaders of the political parties.[4] Twenty years later still, the comprehensive reform plan which had gained ground on the golf-links

---

[1] See Lord Longford's revelations at 518 HL Debs. 606 (25 Apr. 1990).

[2] In *House of Lords Reform*, Cmnd. 3799 (1968).

[3] *Report of the Conference on the Reform of the Second Chamber*, Cd. 9038 (1918).

[4] *Agreed Statement on the Conclusion of the Conference on the Parliament Bill 1947*, Cmd. 7380 (1948).

was placed before the House of Commons in the Parliament (No. 2) Bill, only to have backbenchers from both sides ensure its ignominious withdrawal.[5] Subsequently the political parties went their separate ways. The Conservatives decided that doing nothing was (and still is) the best policy, the party leadership declining to adopt the scheme put forward by Lord Home and a Conservative Party committee in 1978 for a partly nominated and partly elected second chamber.[6] The Liberal Democrats, true to their radical traditions—exemplified in the preamble to Asquith's Parliament Act—wish to see a second chamber elected by proportional representation and possessing major legislative powers.[7] By the late 1970s the Labour Party had abandoned the two-writ scheme and had plumped for complete abolition of the House of Lords, a flirtation with unicameralism which was in its turn ditched in 1989. In that year the party opted to introduce an elected second chamber with limited legislative authority.[8] But now the Labour Government intends to reform the House of Lords in two stages.[9] In the first, the hereditary peers would be removed from membership, if necessary by relying on the Parliament Acts to overcome any intransigence from Conservative and other peers. That would leave an interim House made up of life peers (some worthy hereditaries having been given life peerages to continue their membership). No one political party would have a majority in that interim chamber, and fresh creations of life peers would be recommended over a period of years so that the House would more accurately reflect the votes cast for the various parties at the 1997 general election. Then a joint committee of both Houses would set to work on the second stage of reform, to devise a scheme for a democratically elected second chamber. The Labour Government has clear electoral authority for that process, resulting from its

---

[5] For the text of that Bill see R. Brazier, *Constitutional Texts* (Oxford: Clarendon Press, 1990), 529–40.

[6] For the Conservatives' case see the then Leader of the House of Lords, Viscount Cranborne, at 573 HL Debs. 1581–89 (4 July 1996).

[7] See *Here We Stand: Proposals for Modernizing Britain's Democracy*, Liberal Democrat Federal White Paper No. 6 (London, 1993).

[8] See Ch. 3.

[9] See Labour's manifesto *New Labour: Because Britain Deserves Better* (London: Labour Party, 1997).

manifesto pledge and its landslide general election victory in 1997. But there was no mention of House of Lords reform in the new Government's first Queen's Speech: was it being held back as a silent threat to the peers to behave themselves over the Government's legislative programme?

Over the years paper plans have been supplemented by legislative action over the composition and powers of the House of Lords—not, indeed, of a comprehensive or radical kind, but piecemeal and useful nonetheless. So the House of Commons was made pre-eminent in legislation, and omnipotent over money, by the Parliament Act 1911. After the invention of life peerages in 1958, the House of Lords gradually changed from being a thinly attended and rather sleepy place into a chamber with an average daily attendance of some 300 members which gets through a substantial amount of work. That transformation was enhanced by the introduction of attendance, travel, and office allowances and expenses. Peeresses in their own right and Scottish peers have been full members since 1963, in the same year in which it became possible for hereditary peers to disclaim their peerages for life.[10] None of that has, however, touched the central anachronism that one House of Parliament has a large majority of members who are there only because they are the children of their parents, or who can claim some other line of descent in the hereditary peerage. The House is unelected, unrepresentative, and unaccountable. Why, in a century in which democracy has burgeoned and flourished around the whole world, has the seemingly indefensible survived?

Those who have grappled with the problem of Lords reform might sympathize with Trollope's Plantagenet Palliser. He brought to politics, as seen through the Palliser novels, a burning passion to decimalize the Victorian currency. He failed. As Trollope put it, 'When in power, he had not succeeded in carrying his measure, awed, and at last beaten, by the infinite difficulty in arranging its details.'[11] Lords reform has beaten thus far both Liberal and Labour Ministers, partly because of the complexities of arranging its details, but perhaps mainly because of a number of peculiarities and paradoxes which

[10] See Life Peerages Act 1958, Peerage Act 1963.
[11] A. Trollope, *Phinea Redux* (London, 1874), ch. 1.

beset the upper House. Thus the hereditary composition of the House of Lords was stated to be temporary in the Parliament Act 1911, but it has remained permanent. The United Kingdom has exported to the nations of the Commonwealth large numbers of second chambers based on election, but she has been unable to create one for herself. Everyone (apart from unicameralists) believes that the House of Lords rightly has the power to delay Commons Bills in appropriate circumstances so that (for example) public opinion may be sounded on them; in effect, reliance is placed on an unelected and unrepresentative House to frustrate the wishes of the very chamber which is elected in order to represent public opinion. The government majority in the House of Commons damns hereditary and nominated peers when they delay Commons Bills, but no House of Commons has been able to agree on how to replace such peers with elected representatives. Oppositions want the House of Lords to act against legislation passed at the request of an elective dictatorship, but do not want peers to interfere with *their* legislation when *they* are in office. Many Members of Parliament would like to see a reformed second chamber, provided that it did not exercise its new powers as a rival to the House of Commons; but a newly created second chamber would fairly assume that it had been given powers in order to use them from time to time. A reconstituted second chamber could not be elected by the same method and at the same time as the House of Commons, because it would then be a pointless duplicate of that House; but it could not be elected by a different method and at different times either, because that could result in a chamber with a political make-up different from that of the Commons, thus making conflict between the two Houses inevitable. If the second chamber were to be elected by proportional representation, the objection that is currently made that the House of Lords has no political legitimacy would disappear; but if it *were* so elected the new House would have *greater* political authority and be more representative than the Commons which is merely elected by the first-past-the-post method. In view of all that, if Plantagenet Palliser had been given the option by his creator of either grappling with such peculiar traits and paradoxes or of trying to decimalize the currency, might he not still have elected to pit his wits against pounds, shillings, and pence?

## Bicameralism, Criticisms, and Schemes

Most liberal democracies have legislatures consisting of two chambers.[12] Those that do not usually have small populations, such as Denmark, Sweden, or New Zealand. Even states which have been forced to embark on radical constitutional rearrangements, like Germany after the Second World War (and, indeed, in 1990), or France in 1958, have generally retained a second chamber. Perhaps that trend is explained as much by the forces of inertia and tradition as by any need to provide a legislative check on the lower chamber. Again, most second chambers are elected in one way or another, but in a minority of states some members are appointed by the government and a few are entirely composed in that manner. The United Kingdom goes with the trend in being a bicameralist state; and the House of Lords on an average day, made up of a majority of peers who have been nominated to be there, is not a unique place in the parliaments of the world. What, of course, does make it unique is its potential majority of hereditary members who could turn up to alter the course of its proceedings. The question which should be addressed is not whether the House of Lords is unusual among world legislatures, but whether it is an effective and appropriate part of the parliament of a democratic country approaching the year 2000.

It is possible to state the functions of the House of Lords with some precision, largely as a result of the deliberations of the several inquiries which have investigated it. The 1968 White Paper, for example, listed seven functions.[13] Undoubtedly the most important work of the Lords today is in its consideration and revision of public Bills sent up from the Commons. That work accounts for at least half of peers' time each session, and on average about 1,500 amendments are made by them every year. This is work well done, in that

---

[12] For the historical reasons, see D. Shell's excellent *The House of Lords* (Hemel Hempstead: Philip Allan, 1988), 1–9. And for first-rate general analysis of the issues involved in changing the second chamber see Constitution Unit, *Reform of the House of Lords* (London, 1996).

[13] Cmnd. 3799 (1968). They were: (*a*) to be the supreme court of appeal; (*b*) to provide a forum for debates; (*c*) to revise public Bills passed by the Commons; (*d*) to initiate less controversial public legislation; (*e*) to consider subordinate legislation; (*f*) to scrutinize the activities of the executive; (*g*) to consider private legislation.

the vast majority of Lords amendments are accepted by the government and the House of Commons—unsurprisingly, as most of them are proposed by Ministers in the Lords.[14] The legislative work of the House is complemented by the introduction there each session of about a dozen, usually uncontroversial, government Bills. This reduces the pressure on the Commons, and gives work to peers while they wait for the first Commons Bills of the session to be sent up. The government faces scrutiny through questions from peers, and through Lords select committees, of which those on the European Union and on science and technology are generally acknowledged to be outstanding successes. It is often claimed that the quality of debate in the House of Lords is higher than that in the Commons, a claim which in its nature cannot be proved. Debates are certainly of a *different* quality—much less party-political, joined by experts from many walks of life, not in general constrained by worries about whether a particular speech or point might upset the Whips, or might help or hinder the speaker's hopes for ministerial office. All this scarcely represents a picture of an otiose second chamber, but rather describes one which contributes usefully to the shape of legislation and to discussions of the issues of the day.

But critics of the House of Lords will no doubt come back to the central question of how appropriate it is in a democracy to have a chamber which is dominated by hereditary and mainly Conservative peers. In that form, that is a loaded question which like all good loaded questions asserts rather more than is compatible with the facts. Fifty years ago, the party composition of the House of Lords gave the Conservatives some 400 adherents, the Liberals eighty, and Labour a mere fifteen.[15] Today, that party mix is very different. Leaving out of account those peers with leave of absence and those who have no writ of attendance, the Conservatives can still claim some 480 supporters, while Labour has 126, and the Liberal Democrats 55. But another crucial difference from half a century ago is that there are currently about 325 cross-benchers, who on paper

---

[14] In the 1988–9 session, the House of Lords made 2,401 amendments to Bills, all but a handful of which were acceptable to the Commons: Lord Belstead, Leader of the House of Lords, at 518 HL Debs. 634 (25 Apr. 1990).

[15] See Shell, *The House of Lords*, 13.

at any rate hold a balance of power in the House between any likely government and any likely Opposition. Of course, nothing like the maximum possible complement of some 1,100 peers, or anything like the maximum total of 780 hereditary peers, ever present themselves. The average daily attendance is about 300, in which life peers and hereditary peers of first creation usually have a small majority over hereditary peers. In that working House the Conservatives will be able to count on a small majority.[16] This transformation from a House overwhelmed by hereditary Conservatives has been achieved by the inspired invention and conferment of life peerages.

Thus the House of Lords is not daily dominated by hereditary and, in the main, Conservative peers. But what of the backwoodsmen, caricatured as living deep in the shires, Conservative to a man, and ever ready to answer the summons from the Conservative Chief Whip to sweep to Westminster to save the nation—or at least to save the Conservative Party? The old, and largely accurate, jibe was that the House of Lords snoozed while a Conservative was in Downing Street, but sprang to life to thwart policies of Liberal, and later of Labour, Prime Ministers. Certainly some policies of Labour governments have been delayed (or worse) by the Lords in fairly recent memory: the fates of measures such as the House of Commons (Redistribution of Seats) Bill in 1969, or of the Aircraft and Shipbuilding Industries Bill in 1975–7, or of the Trade Union and Labour Relations (Amendment) Bill in 1975–6, all testify to that. But since the advent of Mr Edward Heath's Government the House of Lords has interfered with Conservative measures, too. It did so most spectacularly over the Bill to cancel Greater London Council elections in 1984 (the unelected House thwarting the elected chamber for acting undemocratically—another paradox), and over the War Crimes Bill in 1990. Although bare statistics about legislative defeats show nothing of their nature or importance, who would have even dreamt in 1979 that by 1989 Mrs Thatcher's Bills would have been amended against her wishes in the House of Lords on 125 occasions?[17] (The Conservative Government suffered its two-hundredth legislative defeat in 1992.) Labour governments have endured

---

[16] See the Conservative Government's figures at 451 HL Debs. 149 (26 Apr. 1984).
[17] Lord Belstead at 146 HL Debs. 534 (6 Nov. 1989).

numerically more setbacks, it is true, but at least a degree of greater even-handedness with respect to both parties seems to have come about. The House of Lords can claim with some justice that it has forced governments of both colours to think again over some of their legislation, in a proper exercise of the powers enshrined in the Parliament Acts. Moreover, it is also important to keep the exercise of the Lords' revising function in proportion. In an average session, almost regardless of which party is in government, about half of public Bills brought from the Commons are passed by the House of Lords with no amendments of any kind.

That Conservative as well as Labour governments are vulnerable to checks in the House of Lords from time to time may be explained by several factors. The number of cross-benchers has increased, and cross-bench peers can act truly independently. The power of party in the second chamber is much weaker than in the Commons, partly because peers cannot be cajoled or disciplined in the same way as their Commons counterparts. In recent years peers have been lobbied more intensely than ever before, because lobbyists believe that amendments are more likely to be carried in the Lords than in the heavily whipped Commons. As a consequence of all this, rhetoric about the uniquely anti-left nature of the modern House of Lords has a rather old-fashioned ring. Certainly, the Government Chief Whip in a Conservative administration can mobilize battalions of peers rarely seen at Westminster to vote the government line. He did so notoriously in 1988 to defeat a vital amendment (moved by a Conservative backbench peer) which would have related the planned poll tax to a person's ability to pay: the second-highest turn out of peers this century ensured a Government victory by 317 votes to 183. Thirty-one peers who voted in the division had not made their maiden speeches, and all but three of them voted with the Government. The Government Chief Whip claimed in the aftermath of that vote that, because attendance at the House of Lords is voluntary, he could only rely on a three-line whip being answered adequately if he were to send it out no more than twice a year. An ability to do even that, so as to bring in so many relative strangers to the House to do the Conservative Party's bidding, is twice more than is justifiable.

What are the main benefits which are conferred on the constitution by the House of Lords? I will pick out two. One is the presence of life peers. People outside the practice of politics, especially men and women rising in their careers, can be inducted into Parliament without having to become professional politicians or to embrace the burdens of elections and constituents. People earning their living, or living and working away from London, are not going to be attracted to Parliament if they have to commit themselves to being there regularly, and the paraphernalia of elections and the demands of constituents would scarcely be an added incentive. The expertise which they possess would not, by and large, be available in Parliament if the second chamber were based on any elective principle. (Whether the mechanism of life peerages is adequately used to bring in sufficient numbers of younger people, women, and representatives of minority groups and of all the regions of the United Kingdom, is another question which will be addressed later.) The other benefit is the unpredictability of the House of Lords in the matter of legislation. In its tendency to treat the legislation of both parties with something approaching an impartial rigour, the House of Lords has become the only counterweight in the British constitution to elective dictatorship.[18] While the government can, in general, rely on the Commons to do as it is told, Ministers have no such felicity in relation to the Lords (although it is right that the elected House should normally get its way in the end). It would be very different if the second chamber were elected. Presumably if one party then held sway in both Houses, Ministers could sleep soundly at night in the knowledge that their Bills were sure of safe passages through Parliament; but when different parties dominated each House, disagreements between the two chambers would inevitably delay the government's legislative programme.

Yet in three major respects the authority of the House of Lords is weakened. It is anomalous, unrepresentative, and Conservative-led. No modern state seeking to create a new legislature would devise anything as odd as a House most of whose members sat on the basis of heredity, while the rest existed on the unrestricted patronage of

[18] The incorporation into domestic law of the European Convention on Human Rights may add an additional counterweight: see Ch. 8.

the head of government. True, the accidents of heredity can produce some young peers: in a survey some years ago, seventy hereditary peers were listed as being under 40 (and over half the hereditary peers were under 60), whereas no life peer was under 40, and only thirty-nine were under 60: indeed, the average age of life peers was 70.[19] But it is not convincing to assert that, because they do not owe their place in Parliament to prime-ministerial patronage, hereditary peers must be independent, for although some are, others are as slavishly devoted to their parties as any recipient of a Prime Minister's favour. The fact that heredity has thrown up a Communist baron (the second Lord Milford) needs to be set against the more important facts that the majority of hereditary peers would usually support the Conservative Party, and that only about a dozen of them take the Labour Whip. Being an unelected House, it is not designed to be representative, but it is not even loosely representative of society. The House of Lords is dominated by well-off, well-educated men: it is not a cross-section of society, in the sort of way that we like to think that juries are. The greatest source of new personnel is the House of Commons, former Members being translated there as life peers for a kind of semi-retirement. The principle of having life peers is defensible: the way in which they are chosen is not. The repeated requests to Mrs Thatcher and to Mr Major from Labour Leaders of the Opposition for the creation of more life peers to reinforce Labour's thin ranks either were refused, or were agreed to but each time in a list containing more Conservative creations than Labour ones. (Indeed, during their premierships 165 Conservative peers were created but only ninety-eight Labour ones. Not surprisingly, the new Labour Prime Minister in 1997 recommended the creation of thirty-one Labour life peers in a single list, along with eleven Liberal Democrat and five Conservative creations.) It cannot be right that one party is permanently in a stronger position in the House of Lords than any other, even if that does not guarantee the sanctity of all Conservative legislation in that House. The Labour Government's 1997 manifesto commitment to end the domination by any one party of the existing House of Lords is warmly to be welcomed.

[19] Figures from 1982 compiled by Shell, *The House of Lords*, 40. The average age of all peers in that year was 63.

So what is to be done about the House of Lords? Since the Labour Party abandoned a policy of abolition in 1989, we are all bicameralists. Abolition of the second chamber would not be a sensible way forward. Without a second chamber, elective dictatorship would be unfettered. Legislation, moreover, would become even worse than it is now: even at its present rate of overworking, the House of Commons manages to pass badly written legislation, tracts of which are immunized against debate and amendment by the guillotine. When he was Leader of the House of Commons, Mr Richard Crossman estimated that if the House of Lords were abolished at least two additional stages would be needed in the Commons to deal adequately with legislation. Meshing in such stages scarcely seems feasible: a second, revising chamber of some sort is, as most other states believe, essential.

At the other extreme from the option of abolition is the Conservative Party's policy of doing absolutely nothing about the Lords. (That is not entirely fair: during her premiership Mrs Thatcher did, after all, revive to a limited degree the practice which had lain discarded for twenty years of recommending the conferment of hereditary peerages.) Mrs Thatcher treated the Home Committee proposals[20] with the same indifference which she showed to most other institutional reforms. Even the mauling by the Lords of the Bill to cancel Greater London Council elections, and the rejection of the War Crimes Bill, did not goad her into action.

Without doubt the most radical scheme for reform emanates from the Liberal Democrats. There should, in their view, be a new Senate, which would consist of about 100 members, directly elected (naturally enough) by proportional representation. Scotland, Wales, Northern Ireland, and each of the English regions would return specified numbers of Senators, each of whom would serve for six years and with one-third retiring every two years. Commons Ministers would attend and participate as appropriate but without

[20] *The House of Lords: Report of the Review Committee* (London: Conservative Political Centre, 1978). It recommended a second chamber of about 400 members, one-third nominated by the Prime Minister after consultation with a committee of Privy Councillors, and two-thirds elected by proportional representation, with the same delaying powers as at present.

votes in Senate proceedings. As would befit such an illustrious body, substantial powers would be vested in it: indeed, the present suspensory veto of about a year possessed by the Lords would, in this Senate, be *doubled*, although its powers over financial legislation would be the same as those of the House of Lords.

That plan would establish a House of Parliament with the political legitimacy which popular election brings. The new chamber would be fully representative of the electorate—indeed, it would be more representative than the House of Commons itself. The political advantage enjoyed over the centuries by one party in the second chamber would be ended. Those would all be notable gains. But the scheme would have certain disadvantages. First, the pool of talented people prepared to make part-time contributions to Parliament as nominated peers would, without doubt, be largely lost, because most such amateurs would have no inclination to turn professional. Secondly, conflict between the House of Commons and the Liberal Democrats' Senate would be unavoidable, at least when the government did not have a majority in it. And lastly the new second chamber would be overwhelmingly party-political, for how many cross-bench members would be elected?

As a first step towards the creation of such a redoubtable chamber the Liberal Democrats accepted, through the Labour–Liberal Democrat Joint Consultative Committee on Constitutional Reform,[21] Labour's two-stage plan for change. So what should we make of the Labour Government's desires to alter the House of Lords? A Bill to give effect to its first wish (to exclude the hereditaries, leaving life peers only) in all probability would be opposed by the House of Lords, but in the last resort the Government could invoke the Parliament Acts to ease its passing. The Conservative jibe is that such a wholly nominated House would constitute an enormous, ermine-clad quango. There is substance to that observation, and such a nominated House would be the more objectionable if the methods for finding new peers remained unaltered, and if the goal of an elected second chamber were not, in fact, achieved. It is also questionable whether (as Labour proposes) a committee composed

[21] See Ch. 3.

entirely of parliamentarians should alone devise a scheme for an elected chamber. This would be insular (for why should not other people have a direct say?), and would be made worse by the Government's disinclination to submit the resulting plan to the people at a referendum (although Ministers could change their mind on that issue).

And so the consensus between the leaders of the three main political parties that was achieved in 1968 has long since dissipated. The Conservative Party has returned to a defence of the status quo. The Liberal Democrats aspire to a strong Senate elected by proportional representation, while accepting that in the meantime the hereditaries should be excluded as soon as possible. Labour wants an interim chamber of life peers, but has no clear idea of what should replace it. Of course, it may be that Labour and the Liberal Democrats will work together on the final solution and—who knows?—perhaps a Conservative Party chastened by a spell in opposition might join them in seeking it. The whole history of attempted reform of the Lords, however, presents troubling auguries: an elected second chamber will be difficult to achieve.

In my view moderate change to the House of Lords is preferable to radical reform. After all, the importance of the second chamber must not be exaggerated. It is much the less powerful and the less significant House. The House of Commons is rightly pre-eminent and is the (admittedly somewhat worn) cradle of British democracy, which needs and deserves all the urgent reformist energy that can be mustered. The fair complaint that the House of Lords caused trouble only for non-Conservative governments has been corrected to an extent. That complaint might, of course, revive, and it would be sensible for some action to be taken soon to make that possibility less likely. Several of the unacceptable incidents of the unreformed House have gradually been removed, such as its co-equal status with the Commons over legislation, its wholly hereditary basis, and its wholly male membership. Attempting to bring about radical change to the House of Lords may simply not be worth a government's parliamentary time and the trouble involved in securing it against the objections of the Opposition; moreover, even if cross-party front-bench agreement were to be achieved, the events of 1968–9 show that such agreement may promise everything yet still deliver nothing. Rather, what should be done, I believe, is to continue in the gradualist tradition of limited and pragmatic reforms, ideally pursued through a Constitutional Commission and with multi-party support.


## A Notion of Reduction

The functions and powers of the House of Lords are the least unsatisfactory features of that chamber. Yet one power is anomalous, the veto which the House retains over subordinate legislation. As this authority has only been used once (to reject the Southern Rhodesia (United Nations Sanctions) Order 1968), it may not be worth worrying about; but an absolute veto, even if restrained by convention, is a disproportionate power. Given the importance of subordinate legislation both in quantity and effect, perhaps the same suspensory veto should exist as for public general Bills. This would be more rational, although because such a change might invite the Lords actually to use such a power from time to time, it would be understandable if any government preferred to leave matters as they are.

It is, however, to the composition of the second chamber that gradualists should turn their minds. Assuming that elections do not reach the House of Lords (as I suspect they will not), the ways in which people are nominated for life peerages are of central importance. The procedures leading up to the publication of lists of working peers hold the key, and, typically of so much of the British constitution, would not require legislation to change them. At present these procedures are informal and based on barter between the parties: the leaders of the opposition parties try to get as many of their supporters as possible accepted for nomination as life peers, while (at least under the late Conservative Government) the Prime Minister has ensured that people who will take the government whip are in the majority in each list. It would be desirable if these discreet procedures could be made rather more formal, and if they could be based on a number of precepts. Thus the party leaders should acknowledge that all the parties represented in the Commons have a legitimate expectation of representation in the House of Lords (subject to some minimum number of Members of Parliament and votes obtained at the previous general election to qualify). They should accept that the active party strengths in the House of Lords, together with votes and seats won at the previous general election, should be taken into account in drawing up lists of working peers. In doing that, the party leaders should try to increase the numbers of non-Conservative peers so as to correct to some degree the historical party imbalance in the Lords. A rough-and-ready formula for replenishing the Lords, with those aims in mind, would be preferable to a descent into tit-for-tat exercises of patronage. Part of a new compact between the leaders ought to be a concerted attempt to find more women, younger people, and members of ethnic minorities for nomination as life peers, together (if possible) with a strategy to ensure that all the nations and regions of the United Kingdom have active representation in the second chamber. There could be a role here for the Public Appointments Unit of the Cabinet Office. The political parties can be relied on to look after their own, but that Unit, if given the Prime Minister's authority, might seek out non-party people, using advertising for the purpose. Voluntary groups and others could put in suggestions, and of course individuals could nominate themselves. Perhaps the party leaders might also agree that certain people should go to the House of Lords by virtue of their offices, such as the Governor of the Bank of England, the general secretary of the Trades Union Congress, and so on. It should not prove controversial to reduce the number of Bishops in the House—for it was agreed in 1968 to cut their presence from twenty-six to sixteen (still a remarkably generous number)—or to try to get leaders of other faiths into the Lords, perhaps ex officio.[22]

What these more formalized procedures should aim at, in a word, is reductions—reductions in the party imbalance in the second chamber, reductions in the average age of life peers, reductions in the imbalance between the sexes, and reductions in the over-representation of the Church of England. This notion of reduction

[22] All of the ideas in this paragraph were published in the first edition of this book in 1991. It was gratifying to see the subsequent acceptance of the essence of several of them by the Labour and Liberal Democrat Parties in their *Report of the Joint Consultative Committee on Constitutional Reform* (London, 1997): see Ch. 3.

might usefully be carried further. Thus the Lords of Appeal in Ordinary, other peers who may sit judicially, and serving judges ought to be excluded from membership. It is wrong in principle that judges are able to intervene in the process of legislation, especially given the growing tendency for some of them to participate in debates on even politically controversial topics. Some legal expertise, which is of particular relevance to the form of legislation, would be lost by their going, but then as it has been estimated that 10 per cent of the House of Lords are qualified lawyers,[23] the loss of even a couple of dozen judicial peers would be of rather less significance than some might suppose. I will argue in Chapter 9 that the proper place for the most senior judges is in a new Supreme Court.

A notion of reduction as a principle to guide changes in the House of Lords ought to apply so as to cut the number of peers entitled to attend its proceedings. Measures must be taken against backwoodsmen, in order to end the disgrace of the attendance of those who are not seen at Westminster for months or even years on end suddenly being called up by the Conservative Chief Whip to outvote those who attend regularly. It is indefensible that a peer who is not able or prepared to present himself for a certain number of parliamentary days should retain his full voting rights. The 1968 White Paper envisaged a minimum attendance requirement of one-third of all sittings each session for voting peers. No one could object to reluctant peers keeping their rights to speak on their rare appearances (although it would be an interesting exercise to see just how many of the worst offenders actually have been moved to add their voices to their votes on such occasions). The Report by the Group on the Working of the House[24] recorded that, counting only those peers who attended at least one-third of the sittings, the party composition of the working House in the 1985–6 session would have been Conservatives 168, Labour 88 and Liberal–SDP Alliance (as they then were) 51, with 73 cross-benchers. On the same basis, there would have been 217 life peers and 163 hereditary peers entitled to vote. The cross-benchers would have held a balance of power

---

[23] Shell, *The House of Lords*, 48.    [24] HL 9 (1987–8), table ii.

between left and right.[25] Now perhaps a one-third requirement would be too onerous, and a lower proportion might be agreed on. It would also be for consideration whether life peers should be subject to the same attendance requirement as hereditary peers. Younger or middle-aged life peers (and potential life peers) who are heavily engaged in earning their living perhaps nowhere near London are to be encouraged, rather than discouraged, from attending or becoming members. A careful balance would need to be struck. An additional advantage of a scheme based on an attendance requirement (or requirements) would be that the leave of absence procedure, invented nearly forty years ago to solve the backwoodsmen problem and having conspicuously failed to do so, could be scrapped.

Given the increased pressure on the House of Lords to carry out its revising function,[26] it deserves to have more Ministers. Those who are there face a fairly heavy burden in being much fewer in number than in the Commons, having to answer for several departments, and having to face many peers (including former senior Ministers and civil servants) who are more knowledgeable than they could hope to be.

A final suggestion is that a Joint Select Committee on Parliamentary Affairs might be set up. One of its tasks would be to try to resolve, in private, conflicts on legislation between the two Houses when they arose. The idea is not new: formerly, a conference of both Houses might have been held in an attempt to settle disputes between the Houses,[27] and the Bryce Committee suggested that the mechanism should be revived. It might prove a useful, though no doubt not always successful, way of reducing disagreement between the two Houses in the matter of legislation.

These ideas will be criticized as being too timid. Certainly, when set against the bold nostrums put up by the Liberal Democrats and by the Labour Party, that is a fair adjective to use. Dreaming up

[25] For statistics on the daily attendance of peers in the 1994–5 session, expressed by party allegiances, see the then Leader of the House of Lords at 572 HL Debs. *17–18* (written answers 8 May 1996).

[26] That pressure would be reduced in the second half of each session if more Bills were to be started in the Lords.

[27] See O. Hood Phillips, *Constitutional and Administrative Law*, 7th edn. (London: Sweet & Maxwell, 1987), 139.

schemes is a simple and agreeable pastime. But, as has been argued throughout this book, reform plans ought to be formulated with the realities of the political situation clearly in mind if they are to stand a reasonable chance of being implemented and of lasting. It may well be that, before the end of the 1997 Parliament, hereditary peers will be deprived of their membership. The risk is that further progress would then prove illusory. What I urge is that the political parties ponder Lords reform together and calmly, rather than separately and only in the light of their own final solutions. If that were done it might be possible to find ways around several noble paradoxes.

# 6  Ministerial Powers

## Ministers and Harlots

A SATISFACTORY definition of the royal prerogative has eluded
very learned men. All the great constitutional writers, including
Blackstone, Dicey, and Maitland, have done their best, but their
attempts have all been criticized on one ground or another. Yet the
notion of the royal prerogative is one of major significance in British
constitutional law and practice, because from it flow many of the
most important powers possessed by Ministers and especially by
the Prime Minister. Decisions on peace and war; the deployment of
the armed forces within the United Kingdom and around the world;
the diminution of national sovereignty through the conclusion of
treaties; the Prime Minister's ability to appoint, reshuffle, and sack
Ministers, to nominate the membership of one House of Parliament,
and to precipitate a general election—all, and much more, is achieved
by or through acts of prerogative.[1]

Statute law is also important. For more than a century governments have derived very many of their powers from parliamentary
authority. Royal prerogative powers have, however, survived the
encroachments of statute—not for the benefit of the Sovereign, but
because they are essential if government is to function. Apart from
special cases where the Sovereign herself may use prerogative
authority in her own discretion,[2] Ministers rely daily on the prerogative for what they do.[3] No one could seriously suggest that the royal
prerogative should be abolished as a historical anachronism. That
Ministers can rely on that part of the common law known as the
royal prerogative to give them authority to do what would otherwise

---

[1] The themes in this chapter are developed in R. Brazier, 'Constitutional Reform and
the Crown', in M. Sunkin and S. Payne (eds.), *The Nature of the Crown* (Oxford:
Clarendon Press, 1998).

[2] See Ch. 7.

[3] For a ministerial defence of the use of prerogative powers see 223 HC Debs. 489–94
(21 Apr. 1993).

be unlawful is highly convenient for them. In relying on the prerogative, Ministers are obviously not limited by the terms of any Act of Parliament. They do not have to pay heed to any safeguards for the citizen which Parliament might have included in any modern, statutory formulation of equivalent powers. They do not have to consult, or even inform, Parliament when they have it in mind to do things by virtue of the prerogative. They do not have to worry in every case whether the courts might review the manner in which they use such powers. As the inability to arrive at a precise definition has shown, the royal prerogative is an elastic concept, the apparent limits of which may be stretched by Ministers; and in doing so they are safe in the knowledge that anyone aggrieved will have to mount a challenge, after the event, through parliamentary and judicial means—if such means are open, and if the citizen has the inclination and perseverance to do so. Once again, an old constitutional notion has proved itself to be exceptionally agreeable to governments. Phrases such as the Queen in Parliament, parliamentary sovereignty, the royal prerogative—all are redolent of the scarlet and ermine of constitutional history, but in fact are cloaks which may obscure the great potency which they give to Ministers.

These comments do not, I hope, echo the absurd diatribe against ministerial power which was unleashed seventy years ago by Lord Hewart, the Lord Chief Justice.[4] Ministers cannot routinely rely on the prerogative to behave like irresponsible autocrats (even if they wished to do so), because there are some restrictions against misuse. Ministers are responsible to Parliament for their actions. The government must be sure that parliamentary support will be forthcoming for things done under the prerogative, just as with things done under any other authority. And Cabinets know that they will be accountable, sooner or later, to the electorate for their stewardship. Even so, for very much of that to be truly reassuring, the parliamentary safeguards against misuse of prerogative power must be such as to cause Ministers to pause and think, and perhaps occasionally to doubt whether they would carry the House of Commons with them. On some great national issues things may, indeed, work

---

[4] In his book *The New Despotism* (London: Ernest Benn, 1929).

that way; but in most other things governments know that the Whips will ensure that all is well, and they know that, over many minor, and indeed dull matters involving the use of the prerogative, Members of Parliament will be largely uninterested in what has been done. In those circumstances, the responsibility of Ministers to Parliament may be merely of theoretical interest rather than a constitutional safeguard against abuse of power. Indeed, it is unquestionably the case that Parliament has permitted the royal prerogative to grant to Ministers, in effect, power without responsibility, which, as Mr Stanley Baldwin reminded us, is the prerogative of the harlot through the ages.

While the legislature has been lax in this matter, the judiciary have stirred themselves, especially in the GCHQ case,[5] so as to place some restraints on executive use of the royal prerogative. The courts will now review the legality of Ministers' use of some prerogative powers. That is certainly an improvement on the citizen's earlier plight, caused by the reluctance of the judges to go beyond determining whether a disputed prerogative power actually existed. Yet even the judicial activism shown in the GCHQ case has not created adequate safeguards. Not every prerogative power is justiciable: matters such as the appointment of Ministers, the dissolution of Parliament, treaty-making, defence matters, and the grant of honours are all still beyond judicial control. Even in relation to those aspects of prerogative which are justiciable, judicial remedies are often available only after the disputed action has taken place. It would be much preferable if some ministerial powers were to be surrounded by procedural and other rules which sought, for example, to ensure that the citizen was treated fairly before his rights were infringed. The best way to do that would be by identifying and confirming those powers in statute, and by prescribing those safeguards within it.

To the interested layman it must seem very odd that, several centuries after most of the royal prerogative was made subject to Parliament, it is still not certain what may be done by virtue of it,

[5] *Council for Civil Service Unions* v. *Minister for the Civil Service* [1985] AC 374. See also, e.g. *R.* v. *Secretary of State for Foreign and Commonwealth Affairs, ex p. Everett* [1989] 1 All ER 655 (issuing of passports); *R.* v. *Secretary of State for the Home Department, ex p. Bentley* [1993] 4 All ER 442 (granting of pardons).

and that so few prior legal restraints have been set in place to curb abuse of the prerogative. But it is not really odd at all. This state of affairs shows yet again that when Ministers acquire power they are, on the whole, perfectly content to keep it to themselves, and that Parliament is quite happy that this should be so. It does not seem too radical to suggest that at least a review is called for, to establish precisely what powers are conferred by the royal prerogative, what legal restraints already attach to them, and what prerogative powers (if any) might sensibly be abolished. Such a review would involve technical legal questions, and the Law Commission would be the ideal forum in which it might be carried out. Of course, Ministers prefer uncertainty in their favour to certainty against them, and it might seem most unlikely that any government would support such a reference to the Law Commission. But it may not be such a utopian and remote prospect as it at first appears, because the Labour Party in opposition committed itself to a review of the royal prerogative when it was next in government. The party recognized the need:

to ensure that all actions of government are subject to political and parliamentary control, including those actions now governed by the arbitrary use of the Royal Prerogative to legitimise actions which would otherwise be contrary to law. [The party reaffirms its] intention to review the Royal Prerogative and to identify particular areas of government activity which should be regulated by statute or excluded from its protection.[6]

That commitment survived the transition to new Labour in the 1990s,[7] although unfortunately there was no reference to it in the 1997 general election manifesto. All praise is due to a major political party for acknowledging that a problem exists with the prerogative, and for proposing a review which could cause Ministers considerable inconvenience if changes were to result from it. And yet I must repeat the criticism made in Chapter 2, and apply it to this particular commitment: a constitutional problem has been identified, but once again it is safe to assume that inappropriate methodology would be proposed to examine and resolve it. On the basis of the

[6] *Meet the Challenge: Make the Change* (London: Labour Party, 1989), 56.
[7] *A New Agenda for Democracy* (London: Labour Party, 1993), 33.

passage just cited, the plan might be to conduct the review through an internal, departmental investigation (perhaps in the Home Office), or possibly through a departmental committee of inquiry. There is no suggestion that any other means would be deployed. I again put in a plea for the use of a body such as my suggested Constitutional Commission.[8] At the heart of these technical questions about the present scope of the royal prerogative are important issues of constitutional power. The proper delimitation of constitutional power is a matter of such importance that it ought to be resolved, wherever possible, on a multi-party basis. The first, technical stage of any review should be carried out by experts, such as those at the Law Commission; then, ideally, its preparatory work should be carried forward by a group such as the suggested Constitutional Commission. The Constitutional Commission might endorse the abolition of any obsolete prerogative powers recommended by the Law Commission: candidates are several, and include the cataleptic prerogative powers to impress men into the Royal Navy, and to create courts to administer the common law. The Constitutional Commission might also identify and confirm that handful of powers which the Sovereign should retain in her personal discretion, such as the appointment of the Prime Minister, and the dissolution of Parliament.[9] By far the greatest burden of work, however, would be borne in deciding how all those other prerogative powers, which are necessary for efficient government, might be reformulated in modern language, in statute, and be made subject, where appropriate, to new safeguards. While the Interception of Communications Act 1985 should not by any means be held up as a perfect model, the process of making prerogative powers subject to statutory limitations which is illustrated by the enactment of that Act at least indicates the general approach. The legally doubtful power of a Secretary of State to issue warrants under the royal prerogative to allow telephone-tapping and to permit the interception of mail has been confirmed in that Act, but has been made subject both to the satisfaction of criteria upon which any warrant may be issued, and to policing by a statutory Tribunal and a Commissioner. (I do not think for a moment

---

[8] On which see Ch. 2.    [9] These powers will be considered further in Ch. 7.

that those safeguards adequately protect the citizen against improper interference with his rights; but it is the *process* which is relevant.) In the more comprehensive review and reformulation of the royal prerogative which I am suggesting, it would be much better if each particular prerogative power were expressly abolished, and any equivalent power and attendant safeguards were enacted. Doubts which have surrounded more ambiguous statutory interventions into prerogative ought thereby to be avoided,[10] and the courts could then be relied on to keep Ministers within the four walls of the new statutory powers. A process of technical, legal review, followed by a multi-party consideration of what powers, currently based on the royal prerogative, should continue to exist, all culminating in the enactment of perhaps a number of statutes precisely defining the continued powers and subjecting them to safeguards, should produce a proper balance between appropriate ministerial authority and the rights of the citizen.

I want to turn now to the personal powers of the Prime Minister. Most of the powers to be discussed derive from the royal prerogative, while the others are based on constitutional convention and political practice.

Every Prime Minister needs, and is entitled to have, a degree of personal authority over his government. He must, for instance, be able to reconstruct the administration from time to time so as to bring in new blood, or to fill posts quickly following a sudden resignation, or to promote people who seem to have ministerial potential. As in any large organization, someone must provide a sense of direction and momentum, and in a government that can only be done by the Prime Minister. To do all this, and much more, a Prime Minister needs personal authority, which is amply given to him by the British constitution. But his personal power is enhanced by other things, too. The Prime Minister's profile is much higher than that of any other Minister. The Prime Minister is frequently news. He has the chance to shine once a week at Prime Minister's Questions, and his shining may be seen on television. His visits and speeches in the country, enhanced by carefully arranged photo-opportunities, con-

---

[10] For these doubts and difficulties, see S. A. de Smith and R. Brazier, *Constitutional and Administrative Law*, 7th edn. (London: Penguin Books, 1994), 144–5.

centrate attention on his doings and sayings. His many visits abroad representing the United Kingdom, meeting major political leaders, attending European Council gatherings, economic summits, biennial Commonwealth heads of government meetings, and so on, all mean that the electorate may be forgiven for concluding that the Prime Minister *is* the government.

It would be silly to suggest that matters of personality and style would be amenable to much change through new constitutional rules. None the less, post-war Prime Ministers have acquired disproportionate power in relation to the House of Commons and to the Cabinet. To adapt the famous 1780 resolution of the House of Commons tabled by George Dunning, the influence of the Prime Minister has increased, is increasing, and ought to be diminished. Who would seek to controvert such a sentiment, other than (no doubt) any Prime Minister? Indeed, an alarming picture can be painted of the consequences of that power, and Mr Tony Benn, notably, has painted it in vivid colours.[11] His canvass shows that Prime Ministers have used prerogative powers so as, for example, to invite United States military forces to be based in the United Kingdom (Mr Clement Attlee in 1945), to commit troops to battle (Sir Anthony Eden and Suez in 1956, to which may be added Mrs Margaret Thatcher and the Falklands in 1982, and Mrs Thatcher and Mr John Major and the Gulf in 1990–1), to conclude treaties of the highest constitutional importance (Mr Edward Heath and the 1972 Treaty of Accession to the European Communities), to appoint and sack Ministers, to create peers (827 in the period 1945 to 1979), and to make hundreds of other appointments. Other specific examples which have occurred since he wrote include the banning of trade unions at GCHQ (a ban lifted in 1997 by the new Labour Government), and the giving of consent to the President of the United States to use airbases in the United Kingdom to bomb Libya. It is not necessary to accept Mr Benn's solution—the adoption of a republican form of government with what are now prerogative powers conferred afresh, as necessary, by Parliament[12]—to recognize some truth in his assertion that the premiership in Britain is, in effect, an elected monarchy.

[11] *Arguments for Socialism* (London: Cape, 1979), 125–6.
[12] See, e.g. his Commonwealth of Britain Bill (HC Bill 161 (1990–1)).

I want to select half a dozen areas in which rearrangement of ministerial power would be highly desirable. The first three concern patronage in one form or another; the other three involve a Prime Minister's working relationship with the Cabinet.

## Restoring Cabinet Government

In a draft for the introduction to Bagehot's *The English Constitution*, Mr Richard Crossman wrote that a Prime Minister can liquidate the political careers of his rivals as effectively as any Soviet leader. This was written long before *perestroika* had been thought of, but even so, his publishers (who must have been very nervous souls) insisted that the sentence be deleted. Crossman obliged, and three years later, after Cabinet experience, that deletion was his only regret about the Introduction.[13] The use which is made of ministerial patronage varies from Prime Minister to Prime Minister. Mr Neville Chamberlain ruthlessly excluded from the Cabinet anyone who might rock the boat of appeasement. Mr Harold Wilson engaged in frequent games of musical chairs, although he refrained from removing very many chairs because he was reluctant to see many colleagues out of the game entirely. As a consequence, Ministers in his administration had a tenure of about eighteen months in any given department. While Mr Wilson had mixed motives for this 'constant fiddling' with Ministers,[14] no one could accuse Mrs Thatcher of having been other than single-minded in her reshuffles. After only two years as Prime Minister five 'wets' had been shuffled out of the Cabinet, and by the time of Mr James Prior's retirement from politics in 1984 only Mr Peter Walker remained to represent the liberal Conservative tradition in the Cabinet Room. Fifty-seven people joined and left Mrs Thatcher's Cabinet, and following Sir Geoffrey Howe's cathartic resignation Mrs Thatcher enjoyed a few weeks before her own departure as the sole survivor from the original formation from 1979. It is easy to see that if Ministers have to work hard to master new

[13] J. Mackintosh, *The British Cabinet*, 3rd edn. (London: Stevens & Sons, 1977), 439.
[14] As R. Crossman described it: see *Diaries of a Cabinet Minister* (London: Cape, 1977), iii. 78.

departments to which they are sent, they will lack time to consider and debate the general position and policies of the government. If, in addition, they are ambitious for higher ministerial office, they will also lack the inclination to oppose the Prime Minister's wishes effectively. Taken together, that lack of time and inclination to challenge the Prime Minister must entrench his power.

Although political limitations on a Prime Minister's patronage do exist, must power over colleagues really be so wide in order to maintain a Prime Minister's proper position as chief of government? The Labour Party constrains its new Prime Ministers by the party rule that, when the first Labour Cabinet is formed after coming to power at a general election, places must be found in it for the elected members of the Shadow Cabinet.[15] Labour Prime Ministers have followed that requirement very closely,[16] and although as a consequence they have found themselves with some Cabinet colleagues who are not congenial to them, it cannot be said that this element of democracy in Cabinet-making has had a deleterious effect on efficient government. This is partly because the obligation to elected Shadow Cabinet members does not continue after the first Cabinet reshuffle, and because there are no elections to Labour Cabinets once formed. Should the system of elections for Labour Shadow Cabinets by the Parliamentary Labour Party be extended to actual Cabinets when Labour is in power? Should the Conservative Party adopt elections by Conservative Members of Parliament at least to its Shadow Cabinet? It would not be sensible to restrict a Prime Minister to the extent of electing individuals to particular ministerial portfolios, and the Prime Minister should retain his discretion to decide who should be sent to which department, and over reshuffles within the Cabinet, a discretion which he would continue to exercise on his knowledge of the people concerned and their particular strengths and weaknesses. Practical points would have to be settled before an elections system were to be put in place, including what the relationship would be between Cabinet elections and the Prime Minister's need to reconstruct the Cabinet from time to time by bringing in new men

---

[15] Standing Orders of the Parliamentary Labour Party, No. E.

[16] Although Mr Tony Blair broke the rule on coming to power by not including Dr David Clark, Mr Michael Meacher, or Mr Tom Clarke in his new Cabinet.

and women and dropping others. Cabinet elections would certainly deprive a Prime Minister of one of his most significant powers, and would induce Cabinet Ministers to have greater regard to the opinions of the parliamentary party which would elect them, and less to the wishes of the Prime Minister. The deference towards the Prime Minister which is induced in Ministers and potential Ministers by their complete dependence on him for place and advancement stifles both criticism of the Prime Minister and the suggestion of alternative policies. That state of affairs is inimical to Cabinet government.

When Mr James Callaghan was asked in 1977 to list all the public appointments for which he was responsible as Prime Minister his written answer ran to four columns of *Hansard*.[17] Even that list was not complete, because (as Mr Callaghan explained) he had omitted ministerial, ecclesiastical, and civil service appointments. This is the second area of prime ministerial patronage—the dazzling range of jobs outside the government which is at his disposal. The Chairman and governors of the BBC, the Governor and directors of the Bank of England, officers such as the Comptroller and Auditor-General, the Parliamentary Commissioner for Administration, and the Chairman of the Public Accounts Committee, Regius Professors, members of Royal Commissions and committees of inquiry—all require the Prime Minister's blessing for appointment. In the civil service, senior officials need the approbation of the Prime Minister for appointment and promotion, approbation which Mrs Thatcher used selectively over choices for Permanent Secretaryships. In the Church of England, nearly 400 appointments are made by the Queen on the Prime Minister's advice. In the judiciary, the Lords of Appeal in Ordinary, the Lords Justices of Appeal, the Master of the Rolls, the Lord Chief Justice, the Vice-Chancellor, and the President of the Family Division, all owe their positions to the Prime Minister (although the Lord Chancellor's approval is also most important). Because of her amazing longevity in office, Mrs Thatcher had to appoint the entire judicial House of Lords, all the Court of Appeal, and all the four heads of division. There are, inevitably, restraints on the choices: for example, the numbers which are involved alone

[17] 932 HC Debs. *232–6* (written answers 19 May 1977).

mean that the Prime Minister must rely on advice about possible candidates. But formal limitations scarcely exist at all. An interested member of the public may hear that there is a vacancy in some post or other; discreet soundings may be taken in private, about which he learns nothing; and the next news is the announcement of the name of the person who has got the job. Individual Ministers, too, possess wide powers of appointment. The adoption of numerous new non-statutory principles and practices concerning public appointments, recommended in 1995 by the Committee on Standards in Public Life,[18] is warmly to be welcomed.

There is a case for subjecting most major public appointments to a parliamentary confirmation process. The public has a right to expect that the fitness of candidates to hold important public jobs will be fully and properly investigated by their representatives in Parliament. Members of Parliament are entitled to discover the attitude to the office under consideration of those who might be appointed to it, and, in particular, to explore the nominee's political, economic, and social beliefs where they are relevant. Such a confirmation process could be conducted by the relevant departmental select committee, or a subcommittee of it set up for the purpose, and a report would be published. If a nominee were not prepared to undergo such a process, then that would presumably make the committee's decision easy to arrive at. That sort of examination would also provide a further safeguard against corruption in public life. It would require political firmness verging on obstinacy for a Prime Minister to insist on making an appointment in the face of an adverse report. Governments could not rely on their arithmetical majorities on the departmental select committees to deliver the goods, for the history of those committees since 1979 shows that they do not routinely report along party lines, and unanimous reports strongly critical of the government have been published. Ecclesiastical, judicial, and civil service appointments in the Prime Minister's gift might be dealt with rather differently. Assuming that the Church of England is not disestablished, why should not the Crown Appointments Commission recommend one person directly to the Queen, as the

---

[18] *First Report of the Committee on Standards in Public Life*, Cm. 2850 (1995).

Supreme Governor of the Church, for appointment to vacancies? Why does the Prime Minister still have the final say over which of the two names put up by the Commission goes to the Queen, especially when not every Prime Minister is a good, or even an indifferent, Anglican? Judicial appointments raise much more important issues than ecclesiastical appointments, and they will be dealt with in Chapter 9. The burden of the argument there will be that it is wrong in principle that two politicians, the Prime Minister and the Lord Chancellor, choose the judiciary, and that new appointments machinery is necessary to ensure that, among other things, political influences are seen to have no part to play. Civil service appointments, too, might be removed from any allegations of bias by giving the Civil Service Commissioners a much more decisive role.

A third aspect of a Prime Minister's patronage, the nomination of peers, was considered in the previous chapter. It would be a sensible development if the preparation of lists of working peers were to be shared with the other party leaders, and were to be based on a number of new principles. This would have to come about by agreement: if such agreement were not forthcoming, we could well witness the unedifying spectacle, started by Mrs Thatcher, of each new Prime Minister packing the lists with a majority of people from his own party. If such a pattern continued, the case for more radical reform of the Lords (which in my view is not made out) would undoubtedly be strengthened.

But what of the Prime Minister's relationship with the Cabinet? There are, I believe, three areas in which changes are needed, with the aim of tilting the balance back towards Cabinet government. They concern recommendations for a dissolution of Parliament, the control of economic policy through, in particular, the annual Budget, and the use of extra-Cabinet decision-making.

The Prime Minister's ability to dissolve Parliament has often been described as an important element in his political authority. Of course, if he can avoid it, no Prime Minister unleashes a general election on his party if the government's fortunes are at a low ebb: every Prime Minister naturally goes to the country at the most advantageous (or least disadvantageous) time for his party. That gives him an obvious advantage over the other political parties, who must make the best they can of the election date chosen for them. Leaders of the Opposition imagine themselves reaping the benefit of that advantage one fine day, and so they are unlikely to be attracted any more than a Prime Minister to the notion of having a fixed-term Parliament of (say) four or five years' duration, followed by an automatic dissolution. It is, however, an idea which deserves further consideration, ideally in a forum such as the Constitutional Commission. It may be, for example, that we have all exaggerated the freedom of manoeuvre enjoyed by Prime Ministers in the matter of dissolution dates. Most Prime Ministers since 1945 seem to have worked on the basis of a four-year parliamentary term, and have tried to put their governments in the best possible light within that period. This may well be because it is risky business for a Prime Minister to allow a Parliament to survive into its final year of life, because things might go wrong for the government during that year as the inevitable appointment with the electorate rushes towards it (as Mr John Major found to his cost in 1997). Equally, we might have assumed too readily that fixed-term Parliaments would end the unfair electoral advantage enjoyed by Prime Ministers. Even if there were fixed-term Parliaments, Prime Ministers would undoubtedly use all the other means at their disposal to make citizens feel as content as possible in good time for the automatic general election. On the other hand, perhaps we have assumed that the term would be more fixed than would actually be the case. The House of Commons would have to be given the authority to bring about a premature dissolution in certain circumstances. There would have to be a mechanism for early dissolution to allow a Prime Minister to seek a fresh mandate to deal with a major emergency, or if he had lost the confidence of the House of Commons. The principle of fixed-term Parliaments, and the practical implications of having them, ought to be examined afresh and in depth. The protestations which Oppositions hurl at the Prime Minister's possession of loaded dice should be taken with large amounts of salt, for they would probably be horrified if steps were actually taken which would deprive them of the eventual use of those dice. Only the Liberal Democrats have taken the criticisms of the present dissolution system to the logical conclusion of demanding automatic dissolutions, although the Labour Government has accepted the principle for the new Scottish Parliament and Welsh Assembly.

But what of the present dissolution decision? Fifteen Prime Ministers since Mr David Lloyd George have had the power which he assumed to recommend a dissolution off his own bat without feeling bound to obtain Cabinet agreement. The constitutional legitimacy of a Prime Minister having the sole right to obtain a general election, rather than seeking it on the basis of collective Cabinet advice, has been challenged,[19] but in practice the Prime Minister *can* make the recommendation without consulting the Cabinet. A restoration of the pre-1918 position would not, however, result in such a major reduction in prime-ministerial authority that Prime Ministers would necessarily oppose it tooth and nail, and I propose that the Prime Minister should have to present this advice as the collective advice of the whole Cabinet. In the light of the way in which Prime Ministers have actually made up their minds about general election dates at least since the end of the Second World War, this would not be a very great departure from current practice. Since that time the Prime Minister has consulted senior Ministers and party officials both to help pick a date *and* to involve them in the responsibility for it. Mrs Thatcher's approach was typical of recent Prime Ministers. Before the announcements of the 1983 and 1987 elections she conferred with a group of senior Cabinet colleagues and the Chief Whip; the discussion led to a 'provisional' date, on which she slept; a full Cabinet was summoned the following day to be informed of her final choice (which confirmed the provisional date); the Prime Minister then saw the Queen, and a public announcement followed. It is obviously better for a Prime Minister to involve at least some senior colleagues in the decision so that they are implicated if all goes wrong. (If all goes right, the Prime Minister's political acumen is applauded and few seem to care that others played a part in picking the date.) This process contradicts the idea that a Prime Minister has unrestricted personal power in the matter. If he were in a minority in the consultations, it would be unwise to press ahead despite ministerial opposition: if electoral defeat resulted, the silence of his

---

[19] Notably by G. Marshall, *Constitutional Conventions* (Oxford: Clarendon Press, 1984), ch. 3.

colleagues over the manner in which the decision had been made could not be guaranteed. In view of this process, which has been followed for decades, it would be but a small step for the Cabinet's formal position to be restored in it. The Cabinet has almost as much at stake at a general election as has the Prime Minister: the fate of the whole government, and the fortunes of the party, turn on it and it is not unreasonable that the date of a general election should be arrived at by the whole Cabinet which is so intimately affected by the result. An attribute of traditional Cabinet government would thereby be restored.

The Cabinet's role in the formulation of economic policy is limited by several factors. In particular, the personality and style of the Prime Minister, and to an extent of the Chancellor of the Exchequer, may diminish the Cabinet's collective contribution: the more authoritarian the Prime Minister, and certainly the more successful the Chancellor, the less will the Cabinet feel disposed to intervene in economic and financial decisions. The combination, for example, of Mrs Thatcher as Prime Minister and of Mr Nigel Lawson as a highly successful Chancellor, must have made Ministers content in the main to leave key economic decisions to them. But such a tacit arrangement is not the same as the situation which invariably surrounds the Budget, which is presented to the Cabinet as a fait accompli. The Chancellor's Budget proposals are of major economic and political importance, but, regardless of the Cabinet's relationship with him, those proposals are first disclosed to the Cabinet on the morning of Budget day. There is no time for any significant changes to be made. It was not ever thus. As late as the 1930s, four or five days would elapse between the Budget Cabinet and the Chancellor's delivery of his proposals to the House of Commons, giving ample time for Ministers to suggest or insist on alterations. The modern cavalier treatment of the Cabinet is justified by the need for secrecy: the less time there is between a Cabinet Minister hearing these secrets and their publication, the less chance there will be of a damaging leak. What, however, is so unique about Budget facts as to make Ministers untrustworthy of them? Is the fear really that Ministers either will leak them (in which case, like Mr J. H. Thomas and Dr Hugh Dalton, they will lose their jobs), or will use the information for personal gain (which, in these days of

computerized stock-market deals, might be difficult to do unde-
tected)? The *effect* of this procedure is to put economic and fiscal
policy firmly in the hands of the Chancellor and the Prime Minister.
What is astonishing is that no Cabinet seems to have rebelled at a
system which both calls into question Ministers' honour and largely
removes the Cabinet from a central area of policy. Of course, all
Chancellors frame their ideas within the government's overall policy,
and even during his pre-Budget purdah the Chancellor will receive
submissions from Ministers about his Budget. It is also true that
since 1981 the Cabinet has met early in early New Year for a full
discussion on economic policy before the Chancellor goes into purdah. But why should not the Cabinet consider key Budget proposals
in draft, no doubt enjoined by warnings about the need for secrecy
of information and the safety of documents? Decisions about economic and fiscal measures for the following year are probably more
important than some other matters with which Cabinets are regaled,
and accordingly are entirely within the appropriate purview of
Cabinet government.

   The exclusion of the Budget from unhurried, full, and collective
debate is but a particularly notable example of the way in which
Prime Ministers can remove matters from the reach of the Cabinet.
The use of Cabinet committees and informal groups of selected
Ministers has permitted more general side-stepping of the full
Cabinet. A system of sub-Cabinet decision-making is essential: the
days are long gone when the full Cabinet could adequately deal with
all questions which have to be addressed by the most senior
Ministers. Small groups of Ministers can settle preliminary issues so
as to leave only fundamental points, or points of disagreement, for
higher authority. Yet extra-Cabinet decision-making has undoubtedly enhanced prime-ministerial power. The Prime Minister has
absolute authority over Cabinet committees. He alone decides to set
them up, which Ministers should serve on them, who is to chair
them, and what the terms of reference will be. He may lay down
rules which restrict access from committees to the Cabinet. He can
give committees executive authority. He decides when to wind them
up. Decisions taken by such bodies, moreover, may be tantamount
to final Cabinet decisions, even if they go to the Cabinet for

approval. For a committee will have considered the topic in detail, with access to expert advice; Ministers on a committee will usually have relevant departmental expertise so that respect will naturally be accorded to their views by the rest of the Cabinet; a Minister who tried to reopen at the Cabinet issues which had been settled in a committee could not count on general support for doing so. Mrs Thatcher *reduced* the number of Cabinet committees, but only because from the earliest days of her government she held discussions with small, informal groups of Ministers. Such flexibility has advantages; but the looseness of such arrangements means that prime-ministerial packing of such gatherings with supporters is quite easy, and that the Cabinet—and even Cabinet committees—are circumvented. The use of more fluid and perhaps more malleable informal ministerial groups helped to make Mrs Thatcher even more powerful in relation to her Cabinet, and her example could be followed in the future.

The public is entitled to know the organization of the Cabinet committee system, given its central place in the way the country is governed. But it was not until 1992 that the publication of the composition and terms of reference of Cabinet committees and subcommittees was ordered, by Mr John Major, thus ending the previous complete secrecy which had surrounded them. That secrecy had been attacked and defended for many years.[20] This was a very welcome foray into open government, and one which has been followed by Mr Tony Blair.[21] Mr Major had also directed the official publication in 1992 of *Questions of Procedure for Ministers*, which is the nearest we have to a ministerial rule-book in the United Kingdom.[22] Mr Blair republished it in 1997 as the *Ministerial Code*.

The Cabinet is responsible to Parliament for the government's tenure of office. While some will say that this is a more notional than real responsibility, it might be agreed that the Cabinet is responsible and indeed accountable to the electorate for its stewardship. As a

[20] For these defences and attacks, see R. Brazier, *Constitutional Practice*, 2nd edn. (Oxford: Clarendon Press, 1994), 117–20.

[21] For his committees see 295 HC Debs. *302–310* (written answers 9 June 1997).

[22] The text is given in R. Brazier, *Ministers of the Crown* (Oxford: Clarendon Press, 1997), app. A.

result, all the members of the Cabinet are, I suggest, entitled to take part in all important decisions which they think ought to be decided by the Cabinet as a body. Conclusions of issues by the Prime Minister, or by Cabinet committees, or by ministerial groups, necessary as that may be for most governmental decisions which are not settled by individual Ministers, must often be second-best to a full Cabinet debate. A restoration of Cabinet government is what should be aimed at, a form of government which did not suddenly start to wane in May 1979. The question of whether to risk the government's life by calling a general election, strategic economic and fiscal decisions epitomized in Budget judgements, and other major matters currently decided in the recesses of government in the absence of the Cabinet, should all be brought back to where they ought to be discussed, at the Cabinet table with all the seats occupied.

A technical review of the royal prerogative by a body such as the Law Commission might commend itself to a government. Even the idea of an independent inquiry into the question of what prerogative powers ought to be rendered into statute, perhaps with fresh safeguards as to their use, is not wholly unimaginable. But how realistic is it as a matter of politics to expect reductions in prime-ministerial power in any of the six areas just outlined? A smile will flicker across the faces of former, present, and hopeful future tenants of Number 10 Downing Street at such extraordinary notions as those. Which Prime Minister or Leader of the Opposition would even contemplate the loss of such authority? But such a predictably dismissive response is based on bluff, and it is high time that the bluff was called. The challenge to overmighty Prime Ministers can only come from Cabinets, Shadow Cabinets, and the political parties. No one else, and no other body, can do it for them. Prime-ministerial powers based both on recommendations to the Sovereign to exercise the royal prerogative and on political usage only exist through the acquiescence of those groups. Thus a Prime Minister's enjoyment of many of his powers depends on the willingness of Cabinet Ministers not to exercise their ministerial powers. They have, for example, been willing for the Prime Minister to have a free hand in ministerial patronage, to decide election dates, to keep economic policy in his and the Chancellor's hands, and for important government decisions to be taken away from the Cabinet. The ability of any new-comer to the premiership to have complete authority over the future of his colleagues results largely from the failure of his party to impose rules about the matter. Such rules might, for example, require either elections by Members of Parliament to the member-ship of the Cabinet (as Labour has for the Shadow Cabinet), or at the very least wider consultations within the party about who should be included in the administration.

The ability of a Prime Minister to decide on how the government shall be run results from a series of abdications of authority by Cabinets in favour of the Prime Minister, based on the simplistic notion that the leader must lead. There has been a failure to insist that those who will, together, bear the responsibility for the govern-ment's performance (mainly Ministers, but also the parliamentary party) have a right to a greater say in how that government is con-ducted and how its decisions should be arrived at. It is not the case that the political changes outlined in this chapter are unattainable, or that any Prime Minister would have an unbreakable veto over them. Rather, it is up to those who collectively have the power to decide whether any or all of such changes would be wise, and in the last resort to insist that they be accepted by party leaders and Prime Ministers. If Shadow and actual Cabinets, and political parties, decide to let things go on as now, then that will be an end of the matter. If Cabinets not yet formed behave, when the time comes, in the same craven fashion towards their Prime Ministers as Mrs Thatcher's Cabinet behaved towards her, prime-ministerial govern-ment will continue unabated. As Mr James Callaghan famously said of Mrs Thatcher's Cabinet (although the sentiment could be applied to many Cabinets), 'If they behave like mice they must expect to be chased'.[23] Even the least mouse-like of Cabinets in the past have allowed prime-ministerial power to increase to the detriment of all Cabinets.

Naturally, there are disincentives to such changes being canvassed. In particular, hardy souls who wished to insist on new arrangements would be threatened with the withholding of the patronage of party

---

[23] 89 HC Debs. 1115 (15 Jan. 1986).

leaders. Certainly, if changes such as those suggested were thought to be appropriate in any party, those who sought to bring them about against the leader's wishes would have to hang together, or, most assuredly, they would all hang separately. But any Prime Minister's authority rests in the end on his party electorate and on his Cabinet. In the end, that fact was dramatically illustrated when the Cabinet and Conservative Members of Parliament forced Mrs Thatcher to abdicate. However successful a Prime Minister may be, however many general elections may be won, however apparently absolute the Prime Minister's grip may seem to be on the political life of the nation, that position is only built on the political authority of the Cabinet and of the parliamentary party. We may not see another Prime Minister toppled in that way for decades, but the memory of it should be etched in the minds of all Mrs Thatcher's successors— and in the minds of Cabinets and parliamentary parties. It is up to them to bring about reductions in prime-ministerial authority and to redress the balance back towards more traditional forms of Cabinet government. Mr Major and (up to a point) Mr Blair have arrived at more decisions through collective discussion than Mrs Thatcher did. In doing so, however, they have only restored matters to what they were before 1979. My thesis is that Prime Ministers were too powerful then and remain too powerful now.

So far I have written mainly about matters over which the Prime Minister has authority. I now want to address issues over which the Cabinet and individual Ministers have clear authority. What is to be suggested is that the existing parliamentary safeguards over the use of the royal prerogative for certain purposes should be supplemented by more effective parliamentary and legal controls.

On three occasions since 1945 the Cabinet has committed large military forces to actual or possible armed conflict, although not, in legal parlance, to war. In none of those cases was Parliament formally consulted before the decision to send forces was made. Suez, the Falklands, and the Gulf all received British armed forces on ministerial direction under the royal prerogative power to dispose those forces as the Crown thinks fit. How odd—perhaps bizarre—it is that the approval of both Houses of Parliament is required for pieces of technical, and often trivial, subordinate legislation, whereas it is not needed at all before men and women can be committed to the possibility of disfigurement or death! Speed of military response may, of course, be vital. Indeed, the quick deployment of British forces in the Gulf in 1990 might have been in small part responsible for Saudi Arabia being made safe from aggression. To insist on prior approval of all military deployments would be absurd, especially when Parliament is in recess, as it was at the start of the Gulf emergency. But the commitment of military forces is an act which may have such terrible consequences that the approval of Parliament ought to be required within a specified period. Even under the present arrangements, no British government is going to take the country to the brink of, or to actual, fighting unless it is reasonably confident that it can carry Parliament with it. Any government will need general political support, and perhaps legislation and certainly appropriations, to wage what ordinary people will call war. Of course that is so: and these facts make the proposal all the more reasonable. The United Kingdom needs a War Powers Act, under which Parliament would have to be informed and its consent obtained within a specified number of days in order that the armed services could be deployed lawfully overseas. (Such a rule would also end the shilly-shallying to which all Leaders of the Opposition seem prone in these circumstances in deciding whether to demand the recall of an adjourned Parliament.) At times of military crisis, the parties in Parliament will usually support the government for fear of seeming unpatriotic. But to argue from that that parliamentary support for government action will always be forthcoming is to deny the existence of parliamentary democracy and the facts of history. After all, Mr Chamberlain appealed to his friends in the Commons to support him in 1940 when military defeat might not have been too far off, but even in such dire straits the House refused to do so. Parliamentary backing for lesser military engagements could by no means always be guaranteed.

The relationships between the United Kingdom and other states involve, among other things, the power or influence which other states are to have in relation to the United Kingdom: in short, they involve relationships of national sovereignty. If any rearrangements of sovereignty are contemplated through new treaty obligations,

Parliament ought not to stand like a spectator on the sidelines. Some treaties are highly technical and others are arrived at as delicate compromises after tricky negotiations; no sensible Parliament would wish to amend them, or to pick and choose which parts it liked and which it would reject. But why should Parliament not have the formal authority to approve all treaties in draft before they can, in English law, be ratified and become effective? That would be a simple rule, conditioned in the use Parliament were to make of it by the precise circumstances in which the draft had been arrived at.[24] The government might try to force its way by relying on the Whips, but such methods do not always work. What I am suggesting in these and other areas is a reversion to the days when governments had a proper respect for the opinions of Parliament.

There are, of course, other matters which Ministers must decide through the use of the royal prerogative but which have no connection with the great issues of peaceful or warlike relations between states. None the less they require better regulation than surrounds them today. Just one may be mentioned by way of example: the grant of passports. In any review of ministerial powers, it is clearly for consideration whether the right to a passport should become a right enshrined in statute which contains procedural rules to ensure fair decision-making. Now that the exercise of the prerogative power in connection with passports is subject to judicial review,[25] and now that (within the European Union) citizens are entitled to identity documents or passports enabling them to leave and re-enter the country, this would be a step which should not cause Ministers too much distress.

The use of ministerial powers, whatever their source, can frequently call into play questions of constitutional propriety.[26] Thus the actions of the Minister for the Civil Service in banning membership of trade unions at GCHQ was declared by the House of Lords to be lawful, but many people questioned the constitutional

[24] For an unsuccessful attempt along those lines see the Treaties (Parliamentary Approval) Bill (HL Bill 27 (1995–6) ).

[25] *R. v. Secretary of State for Foreign and Commonwealth Affairs, ex p. Everett* [1989] 1 All ER 655.

[26] See Ch. 1.

legitimacy of her action. It is regrettable that there is not an official voice, independent of government and Parliament, that could provide an authoritative commentary on the actions of government, including the constitutional propriety of those actions. This would require a fuller understanding of the implications of limited government, or legitimacy, or of constitutional propriety, than have so far been established. Such notions could be worked out by a body such as the proposed Constitutional Commission, but, given its suggested membership (which would include active politicians), it could not be the source of any commentary on the propriety of actual government decisions, given the inevitable conflicts of interest and loyalty. But the exercise of Ministers' powers could be tested against a set of constitutional notions which had been formulated in such a Constitutional Commission in some other, quite separate forum, similar, perhaps to the French Constitutional Council. But that is to range too far, too fast. We should all be prepared to settle in the first instance for a review of Prime Ministers' and Ministers' powers in the manner indicated in this chapter, and for the assertion of their proper rights by the Cabinet, the Shadow Cabinet, the political parties, and Parliament itself with a view to a return to the days of British Cabinet government.

# 7 A Constitutional Guiding Light

## Why not a Republic?

THOMAS PAINE described the Crown as 'a metaphor shown at the Tower for sixpence or a shilling a piece.'[1] In this century, the Crown has become a metaphor representing constitutional monarchy, a monarchy limited in the use of most of its legal powers by the force of convention. The Queen, as the possessor of the Crown, performs many legal and constitutional functions as head of state. As a matter of law, her direct or indirect participation is required in a large number of governmental acts, such as the granting of the royal assent to legislation, the making of Orders in Council, the issue of royal proclamations, the appointment of officers such as ambassadors and high commissioners, and the appointment of Ministers by the delivery to them of seals of office. In limited circumstances, the Queen's legal power might have to be used in a direct intervention in politics. No Prime Minister will hold office unless appointed by the Queen and, although the choice is usually determined for her, the choice of one person rather than another could still require the exercise of her own judgement. The Queen retains a number of reserve powers, for example to refuse her consent to a requested dissolution of Parliament. Even if the scope of the royal prerogative were to be cut drastically, as was suggested in Chapter 6, all of those legal and constitutional, routine and reserve, powers would have to remain vested in someone or some body.[2]

The Crown, or constitutional monarchy, should be no more immune to fundamental reconsideration than any other part of the

[1] Quoted in Hood Phillips, *Constitutional and Administrative Law*, 7th edn. (London: Sweet & Maxwell, 1987), 267.

[2] The Liberal Democrats want to see the Queen's responsibilities for choosing a Prime Minister and for dissolving Parliament transferred to the Speaker: *A Parliament for the People*, Policy Paper No. 20 (London, 1996).

constitution. It has no immunity against reform merely because it is ancient, or because consideration of other systems of government might be taken as some kind of attack on the Queen personally.[3] Nor is the wholehearted acceptance of the monarchy by the political parties conclusive of the issue whether the headship of state should continue to be discharged on a hereditary basis. Republican sentiment is said to be weak in the United Kingdom. That is certainly the case, in the sense that relatively few people would vote to replace the Queen by an elected President. Yet there is undoubtedly criticism of royalty, whether as to the personal behaviour of some younger members of the royal family, or the number and cost of royal residences, or to the number of royal and related persons dismissively described as 'hangers-on'. (The Queen's agreement in 1993 to pay direct taxes, and to remove most members of the royal family from the Civil List, took much of the heat out of arguments about the cost of royalty.) It is, I believe, important to state a number of fairly trite points in order to make a sharp distinction between what is necessarily required in a monarchy as part of a constitution and what is not. First, the Queen as head of state has legal and constitutional duties to perform. As with any head of state, the Queen must have the means of discharging those duties. That requires, at the least, expenditure of a certain amount of public money, a supply of information from Ministers to the Queen, and opportunities for the Queen to exercise her conventional rights in relation to Ministers. By contrast, the rest of the royal family has no such legal or constitutional duties, except one.[4] *Constitutional* considerations do not apply to members of the royal family other than the Queen (and, to the extent that he is the next head of state, the Prince of Wales). As a matter of constitutional law and practice, the United Kingdom does not need an extended royal family supported by substantial sums to help them with where they live, where they go, and what they do.

A second obvious point is that in a parliamentary democracy like that of the United Kingdom it is essential that someone or some

---

[3] For a republican's case see Stephen Haseler, *Britain's Ancien Régime* (London: Cape, 1991).

[4] Specified members may be required under the Regency Acts 1937–53 to act as Counsellors of State in the event of the Queen's absence or illness.

body is able to act, if necessary, as a constitutional umpire. There have been, for example, competing claims to political power following inconclusive general elections, and such claims could recur, especially if proportional representation were to be introduced for elections to the House of Commons. They may continue to be settled by politicians themselves, as on the whole they have been, but there can be no guarantee of that. Or, to take another case, there must be a mechanism to ensure that the political parties perform within the constitutional rules. Such an umpire cannot be appointed from the ranks of the players. He or she may not be called upon to intervene very often, but every constitution should, like any Scout or Guide, be prepared for foreseeable, even though unusual, happenings. If the United Kingdom were to adopt a presidential system of government, with the headships of state and of government merged in one person, the functions of umpire would have to be located elsewhere, perhaps in a Supreme Court with the legal power to hold the actors within the rules of the constitution. On the safe assumption that there will be no such merger, the head of state must retain legal powers.

Yet even arriving at those far from elusive conclusions does not address the question of the attributes which would be best for a head of state in the United Kingdom. His or her duties could be discharged by a President, elected directly by the voters or indirectly by Parliament, with the Prime Minister remaining as head of the government. A powerful case can be made for such a radical break with the past. Several points form the basis for that case. One is that it would extend democracy to the pinnacle of the state, sweeping away both heredity as a basis of influence, and any succour which monarchy gives to class divisions. The person elected would enjoy a constitutional legitimacy based on popular or parliamentary will, not on the privilege of birth. Another point is that the creation of a new office of head of state, proceeding as presumably it would from a blank sheet of paper, would require a fresh statutory formulation of the powers and duties of that office. The present monarchical powers, imprecise as some are, with many only to be seen at all accurately through layers of convention, would be replaced by an unambiguous code of rights and obligations, although no doubt along with some discretionary authority as well. Again, the office of President would be supported by such financial and other arrangements as might be appropriate, but no more. Criticisms which are voiced now about the high cost of the whole monarchy would cease.[5] Those would be not inconsiderable benefits from a constitutional point of view. But, for better or worse, the British constitution is not based on logic alone. To abolish the monarchy would require the setting aside of forces which are no less powerful for being intangible. The Queen is, on any measure yet devised, very popular. She remains a potent symbol of national identity, national loyalty, and national pride. She personifies the nation, a representation made glorious through occasional splendid pomp and ancient ceremonial. By the accounts of those best able to know, the Queen has punctiliously discharged her constitutional rights to be consulted, to encourage, and to warn. That would be a hard act for an elected President to follow, and there is little doubt that most voters do not want the Queen to quit the stage. At root, the question is: would an elected head of state exercise the office any better than a monarch? A President would be democratically chosen and would possess clearly formulated powers: but what would he make of them? It could be that his authority was so circumscribed by Parliament that the risk of the President having to exercise a personal discretion would be almost non-existent. The point of having such a weak officer would be hard to comprehend. If, on the other hand, he were to be endowed with as many discretionary powers as the Queen, his political impartiality might well be called into question when he used them, especially if, in an earlier existence, he had been a politician.

In any systematic and fundamental re-examination of the British constitution, the future of constitutional monarchy should be as proper a question as any other. The political parties have refused to touch the issue with a bargepole, no doubt mainly because they recognize the Queen's popularity and consequently fear the electoral unpopularity involved in raising the question. I have little doubt that

---

[5] There would be several consequential matters to be settled, such as the Queen's place as Head of the Commonwealth and as Supreme Governor of the Church of England. On those roles, and for a generally conservative critique of the monarchy, see V. Bogdanor, *The Monarchy and the Constitution* (Oxford: Clarendon Press, 1995), esp. chs. 9, 10.

root-and-branch reconsideration would support the continuance of constitutional monarchy. But that should not preclude inquiry. Such an investigation—never attempted in our modern constitutional history[6]—would be beneficial. It would, in particular, provide the occasion to decide what should be the Sovereign's appropriate constitutional powers, and I will say more about that shortly. It would also allow a clear delineation of the constitutional duties of royalty from the social attributes of royalty; in the process, a cost-benefit analysis might be carried out into the royal family. As part of that, the manner of financing the head of state should be looked at again. Walter Bagehot's injunction that we should not let in daylight upon royalty, because daylight should not be let in upon magic, was uttered in a more deferential age; more importantly, it also confused the social characteristics of monarchy with its constitutional aspects, which is precisely the distinction that I believe ought to be made as sharply as possible.

### Subjecting Power to Democracy

There is no controversy or difficulty surrounding the Sovereign's place in the workaday constitution. Indeed, ample evidence has been published by former Prime Ministers attesting to the advantages which they obtained from the Queen's use of Bagehot's trinity of rights, exercised within the cardinal convention of the constitution that the Sovereign acts on ministerial advice. Yet the Sovereign continues to possess powers which might have to be exercised when no ministerial advice is available, or when that advice is so constitutionally repugnant that she feels obliged to reject it. Those powers are concerned with the appointment (and dismissal) of the Prime Minister, the dissolution of Parliament, and the granting of royal assent to legislation. What I wish to suggest is that, because the British constitution is based on parliamentary democracy (however imperfect that democracy may be), the opportunity for the use of royal discretion in constitutional affairs ought to be cut to an irre-

---

[6] Much factual information, some of it never published before, was produced in the Report of the Select Committee on the Civil List, HC 29 (1971–2).

ducible minimum. To do that new conventions would have to be worked out so as to ensure that political decisions were arrived at by politicians, who would take responsibility for them. Such a process would mean that in a future political crisis there would be no room for criticism that a non-elected head of state had imposed a particular solution on the elected House. It should also enhance the Queen's perceived impartiality as between the political parties, which would be especially important if no compromise could be arrived at by politicians on their own. A guiding light of political decisions, politically arrived at, might largely remove the need for royal power to be exercised on the Queen's personal initiative in three situations: the appointment of a new Prime Minister following the incumbent's resignation on personal grounds; the return of a hung Parliament; and the appointment of a coalition government to cope with a national emergency. I will take each of those situations in turn.

No government would wish to see a repeat of the events which took place in Blackpool in the autumn of 1963, when Mr Harold Macmillan caused his impending resignation as Prime Minister on the grounds of ill health to be announced to an assembled Conservative Party which had no formal mechanism for electing a new leader.[7] While this *démarche* provided high drama for onlookers, it required the Queen to choose a successor to Mr Macmillan based on customary processes of consultation which he activated from his hospital bed, and controversy has surrounded the accuracy of the consultations ever since. The adoption by the Conservative Party in 1965 of a secret ballot to elect its leader, so bringing itself into line with the other parties, was an example (although no doubt an unwitting one) of the guiding light which I am proposing. Now a new Prime Minister will have to be found occasionally from an existing and continuing government. Prime Ministers fall ill, or grow very old and have to accept the inevitability of leaving politics, or decide to retire, voluntarily or otherwise. In such circumstances there is no reason why the decision about who is to take over the reins of the government should be taken by anyone other than the political party concerned, through its leadership election machinery.

[7] See Geoffrey Marshall, *Constitutional Conventions* (Oxford: Clarendon Press, 1984), 29–32.

When that machinery had produced a new leader, the Queen would merely appoint formally the successful candidate as the new head of government. Such a convention is in a very advanced stage of development. After all, in both 1957 (on the resignation of Sir Anthony Eden) and in 1963 the Queen *did* carry out the wishes of the government party, as those wishes were (however amateurishly or inaccurately) represented to her. The convention worked superbly well in 1976 when Mr Harold Wilson announced his intention to resign as soon as the Labour Party had elected a new leader. On the election of Mr James Callaghan, Mr Wilson resigned and his party successor was appointed Prime Minister. And in 1990 it ensured that all went equally smoothly even in the exciting circumstances of Mrs Margaret Thatcher's withdrawal from the Conservative leadership contest. When she decided to drop out of the race she informed the Queen that she would resign as Prime Minister as soon as her party had completed its election for her successor, and Mr John Major kissed hands as Prime Minister on Mrs Thatcher's subsequent resignation.

A practical difficulty might arise in the context of such a convention as a result of party leadership elections being sometimes very slow affairs. It is possible to speed up the Conservative version with the agreement of the leader and the Chairman of the 1922 Committee, and indeed this was done for the 1990 election. But Labour's room for manoeuvre is limited. The Wilson–Callaghan transfer took three weeks to complete—and that was under the old, simple system in which only Labour Members of Parliament had a vote. Today, any Labour election would have to trundle through the cumbersome electoral college. Speed might be said to be of the essence in some cases, a point of view which would certainly have been pressed had Mrs Thatcher been killed in the Brighton bombing in 1983, and it might also be urged if a Prime Minister were laid low by serious illness at a time of national emergency. There is, happily, a way round this problem which would result in the democratically based convention being upheld. During the transfer of authority between one Prime Minister and the next, the Prime Minister's deputy (or, if there were no such Minister, the number two in the Cabinet pecking-order) could be authorized by the

Cabinet to take charge of the government, but keeping only his existing ministerial portfolio. This caretaker would be chosen automatically by his place in the dead or ailing Prime Minister's government. This is precisely what happened in both 1957 and 1963, when Mr R. A. Butler was asked in turn by Sir Anthony Eden and by Mr Macmillan to take over the government temporarily. (Cruelly for Mr Butler, who was a favourite for the premiership both times, the old adage that there are few things more permanent than those which are expressed to be temporary failed to work its magic in either episode.) As soon as the party election was completed, the formal transfer of power could take place. The democratic ideal would be preserved; no government, during the interim, would be without a pilot to weather the storm; and the Queen would remain isolated from party politics.

British electors return hung Parliaments from time to time. It cannot be said that this has caused major constitutional problems in this century. But it would be unwise to brush aside the possible consequences of such an election. The precedents which might engender complacency, such as those from 1923, 1929, and 1974, must be approached with caution. They amount to little more than political accommodations arrived at both as a result of the political realities of the day and the personal relationships between the party leaders. They should certainly not be taken as rule-constitutive precedents.[8] Caution is also needed before suggesting that new rules should be worked out in advance to prescribe both how a government should be formed in a hung Parliament and the circumstances in which a dissolution of that Parliament should be permitted. It *might* be possible to produce such rules by consensus, but the seemingly intransigent positions of the party leaders make the prospect of success seem rather bleak. The leaders of the Conservative and Labour Parties have refused to discuss hung Parliament issues, on the ground that (as they would be expected to say) they would win an outright victory at the next general election. If cornered, they have insisted that in the wholly unlikely event of a hung Parliament being

[8] For a fuller discussion, see R. Brazier, *Constitutional Practice*, 2nd edn. (Oxford: Clarendon Press, 1994), ch. 2; V. Bogdanor, *Multi-Party Politics and the Constitution* (Cambridge: Cambridge University Press, 1983).

returned, the leader of the largest single party would be entitled to form a minority government. By contrast, the leader of the Liberal Democrats—who might hold the balance of power—has followed the stance taken by earlier third-party leaders in asserting that only a coalition government (or at the least a formal inter-party pact) would do in a hung Parliament. In such unpropitious circumstances, the laying down of new conventional rules might prove difficult. Therefore, procedures need to be described which would keep the Queen's contribution (which might be highly controversial) as near as possible to zero. As a consequence, politicians would have to take responsibility for government-making and election-timing in a hung Parliament. What might those procedures be?

In order that the guiding light of political decisions, politically arrived at, should burn brightly after the election of a hung Parliament, it would be important that no precipitate action be taken from Buckingham Palace. The Prime Minister might wish to inform the Queen of the political situation, as Mr Edward Health did in 1974 after losing his parliamentary majority at the first general election of that year. But I suggest that the Queen should take no part in the resolution of the political crisis. Such a royal disinclination would mean that the political parties would be forced to decide what to make of the electorate's ambiguous judgement. In 1923, 1929, and 1974 the party leaders did, indeed, resolve the succession crises themselves. In each case, a minority government was formed. It may be that that pattern would be repeated, or it may be that the parliamentary arithmetic, the personal relationships of the party leaders (or any two of them), the wishes of the parliamentary parties, and of the parties in the country all came together to cause a coalition to be formed. I do not think for one minute that the party leaders would be averse to taking the initiative themselves in order to keep their destinies in their own hands, and an intimation from Buckingham Palace that no royal intervention should be expected would come as music to their ears. Such a procedure could be communicated to the parties at any time (but preferably when a hung Parliament was only a theoretical possibility), and in an informal way (such as by the Queen's Private Secretary explaining it privately to the party leaders).

In a confused parliamentary situation, however, things might not proceed with the practised ease of a mature constitution. What if agreement between the parties were not forthcoming? The Liberal Democrats might insist on their coalition solution, and, moreover, one condition of their membership of it might be that a potential coalition partner change its leader. A Conservative–Liberal Democrat coalition might, for instance, be considered by those two parties to be preferable to a minority Labour government, but from the Liberal Democrat side only under a Conservative Prime Minister other than the current Conservative leader. Small parties such as the Liberal Democrats always gloss over the fact that whether they could bring about a coalition, with or without such a gross intervention in the affairs of another party, would all depend on whether they had the parliamentary muscle to vote down any minority government. It is never easy for politicians to admit to possible political impotence. But if no other large party were prepared to vote with them (because, say, it did not want to risk an immediate, costly general election so near to the previous contest), a minority government might be fairly secure from defeat on a vote of confidence, and a coalition might remain Liberal Democrat pie in the sky. Even if a coalition were to be agreed on in principle between, in my example, the Conservatives and the Liberal Democrats, Labour, if it were the largest single party, might still insist on its right to form a minority government. And behind both of those possibilities would lurk the prospect of a prime-ministerial request for another dissolution of Parliament.

If government formation in a hung Parliament were likely to take more than a few days, it might be common ground that the incumbent administration should continue in office as a caretaker government, overseeing affairs on a care and maintenance basis in so far as circumstances permitted. The political negotiations—especially if they were aimed at coalition—might be lengthy, but essential administration during the hiatus could be carried out by the caretaker Ministers. Speed in forming the successor government would not then be of the essence: no hasty decision would have to be taken by the Queen or by anyone else about the nature of the new government or the identity of the next Prime Minister. While there should be little dispute about that, the decisions of substance might produce differences which the politicians were unable to reconcile. Suppose that a government lost its majority at a general election, but was the largest single party in the new Parliament. The Prime Minister might insist on his right to continue as head of a minority government. The main opposition party and another, smaller party might state publicly that they wished to form a majority coalition. Agreement between all three parties as to what should happen might prove impossible. In advance of any royal action, I suggest that it should be made known on the Queen's behalf that before she would consider taking any action, proof would have to be made public that a coalition government would be viable. There would have to be a copper-bottomed agreement between the prospective coalition partners, including the name of the proposed Prime Minister, disposition of Cabinet offices, an agreed Queen's Speech, and a guarantee that the coalition would not seek a dissolution within a stated minimum time. That agreement would have to be published. These political negotiations would take place where such matters belong—at Westminster, not at Buckingham Palace. If such an agreement were not forthcoming, the Queen should do nothing to obstruct the continuance of the minority administration in office.

It could be argued that, in the spirit of my suggested royal reticence, the Queen should not intervene in such a case even to the extent suggested. Rather, it might be argued that the minority Prime Minister and his rivals for power should resolve the issue by meeting Parliament. If that happened, and if the minority government survived a vote of confidence, that would be that. But would we be any nearer to a solution to the succession crisis if the government were defeated? The precise nature of any alternative government, and hence its parliamentary viability, would remain unclear. Further, the suggestion that the whole problem be deferred until after the State Opening of Parliament would substitute a second constitutional problem for the first. Few things would be more natural than for the minority Prime Minister to dare the opposition parties to defeat him on the Queen's Speech, just as, for example, Mr Wilson did in 1974. If they accepted the challenge (as they did not even try to do in 1974), the Prime Minister would then presumably ask for an immediate dissolution. An inchoate coalition would, however, be in the wings, claiming the right to take over without a further general election. Would ministerial advice be accepted—or would a person who might have the ability to secure a majority in the existing Parliament be appointed Prime Minister?

There is no doubt that a request for a dissolution can be refused in appropriate circumstances. The rub lies in the words 'in appropriate circumstances'. There are three propositions which I think should be considered for formulation as constitutional conventions.

(*a*) If a government continues in office after an inconclusive election obtained by its Prime Minister, and is defeated on its Queen's Speech, any request for a second dissolution by that Prime Minister should be rejected. No such request, in effect for a recount, has ever been made: the precedents all require that the Prime Minister thereupon resign (as did Mr Stanley Baldwin in 1924).

(*b*) If a new government is formed in a hung Parliament which is subsequently defeated, a request for an election from its Prime Minister—his first such—should be granted (provided, as will be mentioned in a moment, he made it with clean hands). The 1974 precedent is in point. Mr Heath had asked for the February election, and lost it. Mr Wilson's request (some months later) for a dissolution was his first, and was granted. The request will be the more apt the longer was the delay in seeking the election, for the government will have been seen to have done its best in an awkward parliamentary situation.

(*c*) If a Prime Minister in a hung Parliament were to ask for an election, even for his first time, in order to forestall another majority grouping from supplanting his administration, then refusal would be right if that grouping actually existed. Such a royal stance would require one of two conflicting constitutional principles to be preferred, one being that the Queen must accept ministerial advice (here, to dissolve), the other being that a person with a parliamentary majority behind him is entitled to be Prime Minister (here, the head of the proposed coalition). In favour of the Queen giving preference to the second principle would be the Prime Minister's improper motive in trying to thwart his rivals, and the existence of a viable alternative government in the existing House of Commons which could be installed without the need for another election.

Inherent in (*c*) is the question of the presence of a viable alternative administration. One reason for the discredited 'automatic theory' of dissolution—that a dissolution must be granted to every Prime Minister in all circumstances—was that its application would avoid any allegation of royal bias. Such an allegation could otherwise be made if the Queen (like Lord Byng as Governor-General of Canada in 1926) were to refuse in the mistaken belief that another government could be formed, and could carry on without an election, when in the event that proved incorrect and the new government had to be granted the very thing which had been denied its predecessor. As with the primary decision of whether a minority or a coalition government should be formed immediately after the return of a hung Parliament, so here the politicians who were anxious to form a new government from the existing House should be obliged to make public an agreed package concerning the majority government in waiting. Nothing less than that would do if the Queen were to be expected to reject ministerial advice and bring about a new government. Once again, such a process would enable the head of state to give effect to the unambiguous wishes of Members of Parliament: once again, the proposed guiding light of political decisions, politically arrived at, would shine out.

Fortunately, grave national emergencies which can only be met by a grand national coalition government composed of all the political parties are rare events. When such dangers have unleashed themselves, the identification of the person who is to lead the coalition has not proved difficult—Mr David Lloyd George in 1916, Mr Ramsay MacDonald in 1931, and Mr Winston Churchill in 1940. If, however, an emergency coalition were needed but agreement on its leader could not be quickly reached, it would be convenient to have in place an understanding of how a new Prime Minister could be chosen through a democratic process rather than through the use of the Sovereign's prerogative. What I suggest is that the House of

Commons as a whole should choose him.[9] The existing government should continue as a caretaker until candidates are nominated and a secret ballot is held under (say) the superintendence of the Speaker. The person receiving the most votes of Members would be formally appointed Prime Minister. Even at a time of national emergency, the ideal of election could still take precedence over royal nomination— assuming, of course, that Parliament were sitting at the onset of the emergency.

Thus far the whole thrust of the argument has been that British parliamentary democracy needs to be made more complete by agree- ments to reduce the potential scope of royal discretionary power to an absolute minimum. The Queen's power to refuse a dissolution has been examined, and procedures have been indicated which ought to ensure that any refusal should have the support of the House of Commons. But the Queen has other reserve powers: to *insist* on a dissolution, to refuse royal assent, and to dismiss a government.[10] These powers remain shrouded in mystery, not because of any legal doubt that they exist, but because they have lain unused for so long. Sovereigns and Prime Ministers have obeyed what they have taken to be the constitutional rules. Governments have not behaved in out- rageous or illegal ways that have invited the exercise of royal reserve powers to check them. Should not the realities of contemporary constitutional and political conduct therefore be recognized by the formal abolition of all, or at least a majority of, those powers? The power to refuse a dissolution might be exempted from such abo- lition, for it might be relevant in some future hung Parliament. I think that caution dictates that the other powers should also be maintained—but, again, I want to suggest that decision-making be diverted to political authority.

Any royal insistence that Parliament be dissolved would throw the final judgement on a government to the electorate, exactly where such judgements belong. If a government were to refuse to recom- mend an election, or to resign, following its defeat in the House of Commons on a vote of confidence, or if a government were to ask for a mass creation of peers in order to overcome an obstructionist

[9] See also Brazier, *Constitutional Practice*, 15–18.
[10] See also Brazier, *Constitutional Practice*, 185–93.

House of Lords, but declined to follow precedent and allow the electorate's opinion to be tested first—unlikely though such astonishing turns of events would be—the Queen would be justified in requiring that a general election be held. Perhaps any case in which refusal of assent to legislation were contemplated might be met more appropriately by insistence on a dissolution, especially as it is very hard to postulate realistic examples of conduct which might invite such refusal. If, for example, a government were to procure the passage of legislation to prolong the life of Parliament for an improper reason, the House of Lords could use its absolute veto to block the Bill's passage: no question of refusal of assent would arise in that case.[11] Or, to take another example, a government might persuade Parliament to pass a Bill subversive of the democratic basis of the constitution which the Queen might feel justified in vetoing in her capacity as the ultimate guardian of the constitution; but she could more appropriately insist on a general election to test the electorate's attitude to the Bill, and leave the question of royal assent until that verdict was available. Vigorous private protest, perhaps followed by a general election forced by the head of state if the government persisted in its plans, would be a safer royal reaction, for it would throw the final decision to the voters. Similarly, the power to dismiss a government might also be better left dormant in favour of a forced dissolution. If a government declined to budge after defeat on a vote of confidence, might it not be wiser for its fate to be decided by the voters at a general election brought about by the Sovereign? (Admittedly, in such extraordinary circumstances, that government might refuse to bow to the wishes of the electorate, in which case dismissal would be the only weapon left to dislodge it.)

Royal power in the United Kingdom is (or should be) the handmaiden of parliamentary democracy, not its master. If understandings along the lines of those outlined here were to find support, the supremacy of the political authority in the British constitution (whether the House of Commons, or the electorate) would be made clear beyond doubt. In highly charged political circumstances the Queen's personal discretion would be made subject by and large to

[11]  Parliament Act 1911, s. (2)1.

the resolution of political questions by politicians. Only if the political process were to fail would the head of state, as final arbiter of the constitution, have to act on her personal responsibility. The working-out of new conventions, and the further development of older ones, would be best done in an authoritative body such as the suggested Constitutional Commission.[12] Some matters would be easier to agree on than others: a clear convention about the procedure to be followed on the Prime Minister's resignation on personal grounds would be straightforward, while the action needed to resolve rival claims to office in a hung Parliament might not. In such cases of disagreement, it would be consistent with my attempts to reduce royal political power if Buckingham Palace were to indicate that the guiding principle would, indeed, be that the politicians themselves would be expected to take the responsibility for resolving any future political crisis, and that accordingly the Queen would be disinclined to take an initiative in it unless and until the political process had clearly failed.

## Constitutional Continuity

A final aspect of constitutional monarchy which needs consideration is the legal relationship between the Queen as head of state and the Prince of Wales as the next head of state. The constitutional status of the Prince of Wales could easily continue for another twenty years or more.[13] He has little prospect of attaining the Crown until he is over sixty, and his accession is most unlikely to be accelerated by the Queen's abdication. Her concept of monarchy as being hereditary, and therefore for life, appears to have induced in her a profound sense of duty towards the throne, sanctified by her vows at the Coronation, and strengthened by the unhappy memories of Edward VIII's quitting of his responsibilities in 1936.

Prince Charles has some limited experience of the role which he will one day exercise as king, through periodic appointment as

[12] See Ch. 2.
[13] See R. Brazier, 'The Constitutional Position of the Prince of Wales' [1995] *Public Law* 401.

Counsellor of State. The appointment of Counsellors of State, and provision for a Regency, are two mechanisms through which the Sovereign's functions in government may be discharged when he or she is unable to fulfil them as a result of illness, absence, or minority.[14] Counsellors are appointed if the Queen intends to be absent from the United Kingdom, and would be appointed if she were suffering from an illness which was not, however, so serious as to require a Regency. The Counsellors have delegated to them such royal functions as are specified in Letters Patent issued for the purpose; they are, however, statute-barred from dissolving Parliament (except on the Sovereign's express instructions) and from creating peers. A Regent would be appointed if a Sovereign succeeded under the age of 18, or if the Sovereign were by reason of infirmity of mind or body incapable for the time being of performing royal functions, or if he or she were for some definite cause unable to perform them. If a Regent were required today, he would be Prince Charles. A Regent could perform all the functions of the Sovereign, except consenting to Bills to alter the succession to the throne, or which would repeal the Acts securing the established Church in Scotland.

The present law was not designed to allow any substantial transfer of functions from a relatively fit Sovereign to an heir apparent so as to give the latter greater experience of constitutional matters, or to ease the burden on an ageing head of state. I believe that a new Regency Bill should be contemplated within the next few years, in order to ensure that constitutional continuity was assured in all foreseeable circumstances. Such legislation could retain the present provisions for Counsellors of State and for a Regency, but it should also permit the Sovereign to put a Regent into office by Letters Patent whenever she thought fit. Such a mechanism should be flexible enough to permit a Regency for specified periods, such as the Queen's lengthy absence abroad; it should also allow her, as old age made it more difficult to fulfil all the duties of modern monarchy, to begin to delegate duties to Prince Charles as Regent. An objection to dividing royal functions in that way would be the constitutional oddity of having both a Queen Regnant and a Prince Regent, when the

---

[14] Regency Acts 1937–53.

former was not incapacitated. That minor difficulty could be met by the invention of a new title for Prince Charles in that role—perhaps that of Viceroy. If this idea found favour at Buckingham Palace (and it would obviously require an initiative from, and the full-hearted consent of the Queen and the Prince of Wales), the Prime Minister and the Cabinet would need to be informed of the Queen's wishes, and there is no reason to suppose that they would wish to do other than to cooperate in preparing legislation. No doubt the Leader of the Opposition and the other party leaders would be told of the development by the Prime Minister so that the changes might receive cross-party support in Parliament.

Possible Regency provisions are not of the first order of importance in the British constitution. But because the Sovereign possesses governmental and other responsibilities, the law ought to be so framed as to ensure that those responsibilities can be discharged as efficiently as possible. The Queen may be naturally reluctant to accept the idea of the Prince of Wales as Regent (or Viceroy), because to do so might smack of a dereliction of her duty. But she might be advised that her duty also includes the need to prepare Prince Charles for kingship, and to lay plans for the monarchy in her old age. Constitutional monarchy itself is not, indeed, of the first importance in the British constitution. But questions about the location of power in the constitution are important, and in this chapter various political decisions have been identified which some person or body must be empowered to take. I have proposed conventions and procedures which would enable those decisions to be taken in a democracy where they should be taken.

# 8 Defending Rights

## Liberty Attacked and Defended

IT was not only Victorian worthies in the pages of fiction who spoke disparagingly of foreign constitutions.[1] The great A. V. Dicey himself dismissed with scorn the way in which the rights of the citizen were defended abroad. As he put it, 'most foreign constitution-makers have begun with declarations of rights. For this they have often been in no wise to blame.'[2] What Dicey seems to have had uppermost in his mind was the futility of setting out ringing declarations of human freedoms without underpinning the rhetoric of liberty with effective means to protect them. To the extent that, in England, matters have always been very different—precise, legal remedies being available through which the citizen can secure his freedoms, but without any general statement of rights—Victorian commentators naturally took it for granted that, once again, England had got things entirely right while all foreigners had got them completely wrong.

But more recently many people in the United Kingdom have come to believe that human rights are now much better protected in many foreign legal systems than they are in Britain. The old Victorian certainties have been swept away. How can this have happened? Two things have changed. Abroad, states have incorporated in more modern declarations of rights highly effective, and usually judicial, means to guarantee that rights are enjoyed against all comers, including governments which might be avaricious for greater powers. Rights have obtained sanctions for breach. At home in the United Kingdom, elective dictatorship[3] has allowed British governments either to be careless whether their legislative and administrative acts derogate appropriately from human rights, or (according to

---

[1] See p. 8.
[2] Dicey, *Introduction to the Study of the Law of the Constitution* (London: Macmillan, 1959), 198.
[3] See Ch. 1.

taste) has permitted governments deliberately to infringe the rights of the citizen in favour of increased power for central government. In my view, although personal liberty lost ground during the last Conservative government (and during Mrs Thatcher's reign in particular), the setbacks to freedom did not start in 1979; moreover, I think that the extent of the loss since 1979 has occasionally been exaggerated. Hyperbole unleashed in the debate about civil rights by those on the political left against the privations of a right-wing government are fair enough,[4] but even some academic commentators have been rather carried away in anti-Thatcher diatribes.[5] Be that as it may, it is now commonly argued that legislative, and perhaps institutional, change is urgently needed in order to improve the lot of civil liberties in Britain.

At first sight the omens in favour of any such reform might be thought to be bleak. Many of those who most need guaranteed and effective rights, such as the poor, or the badly educated, or the unpopular, are the least able to secure them. There may well be few votes to be gained by a political party in proposing an extension of rights to such people. And more rights for the individual mean less power (or at the least great inconvenience) for any government. It is all very well to incant sentiments such as its being a measure of a society's greatness that it accords the same, large, protection under the law to the disadvantaged as to those who have the political muscle to fight for rights; it is quite another to convince a political party to give practical effect to such a sentiment through legislative action. Against such a background both the Liberal Democrats and the Labour Party deserve full credit for committing themselves—in different ways—to extending civil rights.

Of course, to argue that civil rights in the United Kingdom are not what they once were or are not what they ought to be requires some litmus-test against which the assertion can be measured. One such serviceable test is provided in the judgments of the European

---

[4] See the dismal catalogue listed by the then Shadow Lord Chancellor, Lord Irvine of Lairg, in the House of Lords debate on the state of civil liberties under Mrs Thatcher's administration: 519 HL Debs. 904–9 (23 May 1990).

[5] See esp. P. McAuslan and J. F. McEldowney, 'Legitimacy and the Constitution: The Dissonance between Theory and Practice', in P. McAuslan and J. McEldowney (eds.), *Law, Legitimacy and the Constitution* (London: Sweet & Maxwell, 1985), 1–38.

Court of Human Rights, which register strongly against the state of liberty in Britain. By late 1997 that Court had found against the British government in fifty cases. As a result many things which the courts, Parliament, and successive governments in the United Kingdom had accepted as being perfectly proper were declared to violate the European Convention on Human Rights, and action has had to be taken to bring British law and practice into conformity with the European Convention. The regime for tapping telephones; birching in the Isle of Man; discriminatory Immigration Rules; the law on homosexuality in Northern Ireland; the law of contempt; the rights of prisoners; the rights of the mentally ill: all these things, and many others, were in a perfectly acceptable state in the eyes of British judges and politicians, but fell below the standards insisted upon by the terms of the European Convention. The shaft of liberty's light cast by British judges by means of the progressive development of judicial review of administrative action only partially illumines the gloom of those European condemnations.

Many on the political left in Britain claim, not unfairly, that most civil rights have been secured in the United Kingdom by legislation, and not by the courts. They suspect that the judiciary would not develop the law in favour of the rights of the individual, and therefore argue that the parliamentary process should be allowed to continue. In that way further rights must be established through democratic means, and as little reliance as possible should be placed on the judges who, for various reasons, are ill-equipped for the task of securing and extending freedoms. Individuals with grievances about civil rights must, on this view, put pressure on Members of Parliament to change the law. However, in my view it would be unwise to pin all hope on ad hoc parliamentary reaction to such pressure. There are limits on what the individual can be expected to achieve in securing a change in the law from Parliament for an alleged wrong. He is, in effect, being asked to pursue a mere possibility that the government might deem it expedient to take action. Yet it may be that it was the government's own action which raised the grievance in the first place, thus making Ministers judges in their own cause. The attitude of the government's own backbenchers to the situation, the inconvenience for Ministers which might result if it were to take steps to correct the injustice, the pressure on the legislative programme, and perhaps the general unpopularity of the complainant, might very well all persuade the government that no action was the best action. Whatever might have been Parliament's historic place in securing individual rights, the realities of contemporary politics mean that more people look for help, not to their Members of Parliament, but to the courts (especially through applications for judicial review), and if need be to the European Court of Human Rights. Given the choice of an enforceable legal right on the one hand, or the possibility of a legislative remedy on the other, it is easy to see why the existence of a legal remedy is a more attractive option than future legislative action. Applications for judicial review, and petitions to the European Commission of Human Rights, might not have increased as they have if Parliament had been the effective guarantor of rights which its Members, and others, persist in claiming it still to be. Both the courts and Parliament must share the blame for failing to develop civil rights in the United Kingdom.

What is to be done to put matters right? The policies of the political parties are very important, because the party in power sets the framework for the protection of rights. Ministers have the ability to do something about civil rights which those outside Parliament lack. Demands that action be taken to improve individual rights counted for little before the intransigence of the last Government. Everything in the Conservatives' garden was rosy: I suppose that, having been in power for so long, they perhaps viewed things through rose-tinted spectacles. The general satisfactory condition of the garden was due to the loving attention, as required, of judicial gardeners; the occasional weed was removed by parliamentary action; from time to time parts of the display received low marks in the European competition, but maintenance work was then speedily carried out to bring the exhibits up to the mark. Outside that garden the other political parties see matters very differently. The Liberal Democrats believe that radical change is necessary, and urge the incorporation into municipal law of the European Convention, together with the protocols to it, as a new United Kingdom Bill of Rights.[6] The legislation which

[6] For a Liberal Democrat peer's attempt to achieve this see 560 HL Debs. 1136–74 (25 Jan. 1995).

would do that should, in their view, require United Kingdom courts in applying it to have regard to the judgments of the European Court of Human Rights, and to reports and decisions of the European Commission of Human Rights. That policy has been supported for a long time by pressure groups, including Liberty and Charter 88.

The Labour Party has undergone a radical change of mind towards the question of a Bill of Rights.[7] For most of its life the party has opposed the ceding of the protection of rights from Parliament to the courts. In the late 1980s, however, Labour took a tentative step towards a greater protection of individual rights by advocating a series of new civil rights statutes, collectively to be known as the Charter of Rights. That would have amounted to an attempt to pass legislation in detailed language on discrete topics, leaving as little opportunity as possible for judicial meddling in Parliament's intentions. Labour at that time continued to reject the case for a Bill of Rights on the grounds that it could not be entrenched (a point which I will consider in a moment), and because such a Bill—cast in statements of general principle—would be open to interpretation by the judges, with no certainty that they would give adequate protection to the most vulnerable members of society. There was an objection in principle to be made to Labour's Charter of Rights approach. Rights exist—or ought to exist—independently of the wishes of governments. A government and Parliament should not be able to select certain rights to protect, and pass statutes to establish them, while leaving other rights outside the ambit of the law. Rights ought to exist above and beyond the reach of any government, Parliament, or party: the availability of rights should not vary according to whether a particular government finds them convenient, or acceptable, or compatible with its electoral aims. That suspicion of any coherent and comprehensive code of individual rights echoes disagreements which existed in the post-war Labour Government. Sir Stafford Cripps urged the Cabinet not to ratify the European Convention on Human Rights because he thought that its provisions would make it impossible, or certainly very difficult, for the government to achieve a fully planned economy. The Cabinet

---

[7] See Ch. 3.

decided against him, but Cripps's reservations remained in Labour's subconscious for a long time.

By the time of the 1997 general election the Labour Party had committed itself to incorporate the European Convention on Human Rights into English law.[8] In the autumn of 1997 the Labour Government published a White Paper to explain how this would be done,[9] together with the Human Rights Bill to give effect to the proposals. Under the Bill it would be unlawful for any public authority (a concept which was widely defined) to act in a way incompatible with Convention rights. A person aggrieved by such unlawfulness would be able to challenge the authority in the courts, and at any appropriate level of court. The courts would be bound to take account of relevant decisions of the European Court of Human Rights (but these decisions would not be binding on English courts). As far as interpretation is concerned, Acts and secondary legislation would have to be interpreted by the courts as far as possible so as to be compatible with the Convention, a requirement that would apply to future as well as to existing legislation. If a court finds that a rule of statute law conflicted with Convention rights it would not have the power to strike it down, but it could issue a declaration of incompatibility. The Government and Parliament would thereby be placed under political pressure to alter the statute law. Legislation to be so amended could be changed by an Order in Council, so the usual delay in passing an ordinary Bill would be avoided. In future Ministers will be under a duty, in introducing any Bill into Parliament, to declare whether its provisions would be compatible with the Convention.

## A Red Herring

One of the Labour Party's reasons for its former policy of spurning both the adoption of a new Bill of Rights and the incorporation into English law of the fairly old European Convention was that no such document could be entrenched against amendment or repeal. For

---

[8] See Ch. 3.    [9] *Rights Brought Home: The Human Rights Bill*, Cm. 3782 (1997).

others, that is *the* conclusive reason against adopting a Bill of Rights. Much was made of the point in a House of Commons debate in 1990 on a possible Bill of Rights, and for most Members who spoke that was the end of the matter. Every first-year law student knows what Dicey said about parliamentary sovereignty: that Parliament can make or unmake any law whatever.[10] So how would rights in a new declaration of rights be any better protected against the rapacity of elective dictatorship, given that fresh legislation could encroach on the rights declared in it? The government could easily get Parliament to amend, or indeed entirely repeal, any inconvenient provisions with the assistance of the Whips. Now there are several ways in which the entrenchment argument (or rather the *lack* of entrenchment argument) can be answered. One on which I will spend no time is the notion of a legal revolution which, through the adoption of a comprehensive new constitutional settlement including a written constitution and a Bill of Rights, would overthrow the present constitutional order and with it the doctrine of absolute parliamentary sovereignty. As I argued in Chapter 1, the United Kingdom will not experience such a revolution, and so discussing it as a method of entrenching a Bill of Rights is a singular waste of effort. I will, however, summarize five other solutions.[11]

The first is to concede the argument outright and accept that the uniquely odd nature of the British constitution means that entrenchment would, indeed, be impossible. Let it be acknowledged that not only is the United Kingdom Parliament unique in being unable to enact effective entrenched legislation, but also that it is unique in having no power to alter that fundamental rule of the constitution by legislative means. It would be quite possible to leave all of that unchallenged, and to pass a new Bill of Rights as an ordinary statute, amendable and repealable in the usual way, but to include a requirement in it that a Minister report formally to Parliament if any subsequent draft legislation appeared to be inconsistent with the new Bill. (This is what the Government has decided to do under its

[10] Dicey, *Introduction*, 39–40. That view is now subject to the supremacy of European Community law.

[11] On the question generally see the excellent analysis in J. Jaconelli, *Enacting a Bill of Rights: The Legal Issues* (Oxford: Clarendon Press, 1980), ch. VI.

Human Rights Bill.) Such a Bill of Rights might acquire a special place in British constitutional legislation. It might come to possess a moral force of its own, with governments loath to introduce any measure which would derogate from it. The rule that any government wishing to do so would have to declare its intention openly ought to place a particular responsibility on Ministers to explain why they wished to act in that way, so exposing them to criticism and perhaps to political unpopularity. If, as the years rolled by, the Bill of Rights remained unamended (or perhaps amended in only minor ways) it might be protected as a matter of political reality, although not (it is true) as well as if some special method were required as a matter of law to amend it. The House of Lords might wish, as a matter of practice, to keep a special eye on the Bill, and to be ready to exercise its ordinary suspensory veto over any amending Bill if peers were not persuaded of its desirability. Thus the government and Commons alone—even ably helped by the Whips—might ultimately have to resort to the Parliament Acts to amend the Bill of Rights, which would attract additional, and possibly adverse, publicity to their action. As a result, the United Kingdom would retain an unsullied doctrine of parliamentary sovereignty while also acquiring some political protection against easy amendment of its new Bill of Rights.

A second answer to the entrenchment question would be to adopt what might be called the football-pools solution.[12] The new Bill of Rights might contain an entrenchment mechanism, say a requirement that special majorities be obtained in both Houses before any amendment were duly passed. But—as with the football pools—that arrangement would be binding in honour only. The orthodox view of parliamentary sovereignty would remain; as a matter of practice, though, governments and Parliaments might consider themselves honour-bound to follow the amendment mechanism given the special nature of legislation designed to secure fundamental rights and freedoms. If the mechanism were ignored by Parliament on any occasion, that would be a lawful manifestation of parliamentary sovereignty (although, over time, the judges might adapt their attitude to that sovereignty and ascribe to the entrenchment provision the

---

[12] This is my label for a suggestion made by Hood Phillips, *Constitutional and Administrative Law*, 7th edn. (London: Sweet & Maxwell, 1987), 437.

attributes of a binding rule). Parliaments and governments might not wish, however, to incur the odium of breaking the amendment terms of the Bill of Rights, just as football-pool companies do not welsh on winning bets; and the Bill would, in effect, have achieved a degree of special protection which Dicey and others would say was impossible to achieve.

Then, thirdly, there are the various interpretative devices which have been suggested over the years. So, a Bill of Rights might state that any earlier Act which was inconsistent with it was, to the extent of that inconsistency, repealed, and that any inconsistent common law rule was abrogated. It might also contain a direction to the judges that any legislation passed *after* the Bill of Rights was to be interpreted consistently with it, if that were possible; it might also state (to bow the knee to parliamentary sovereignty) that if such an interpretation were not possible, the later provision must override the Bill, as would any later Act which stated expressly that it was to have effect despite any inconsistent language in the Bill of Rights. (Again, that is the general approach which the Government has adopted in its Human Rights Bill.) There is, of course, much judicial and other authority which urges that a line be drawn there in seeking to defend civil rights legislation against amendment or repeal. Both the Standing Advisory Committee on Human Rights in Northern Ireland and the Select Committee of the House of Lords on a Bill of Rights[13] have reported—consistently with academic and judicial opinion—that any attempt (by interpretative provisions or otherwise) to override *future* inconsistent Acts would be nugatory. Even if the line were to be drawn short of such an attempt, a Bill of Rights which contained interpretative sections such as those just indicated would none the less be before the judges frequently and would require them to compare and contrast other statutory provisions with it. It is hard to think of any other single Act to which reference might be made so frequently in court. Older statutes would be checked to see whether they had suffered implied repeal; newer statutes would be scrutinized for consistency with the Bill of Rights; judges would become immersed in the language of rights. That process would inevitably give it a rather special place in the scheme of British legislation.

[13] Cmnd. 7009 (1977); HL 176 (1977–8).

Fourthly, it would be possible to choose a parliamentary solution to the entrenchment problem. One has been suggested by Lord Scarman.[14] He thinks that the European Convention should be incorporated into English law, and that a new Parliament Act should be passed which would give the House of Lords an absolute veto over Bills to amend or repeal that Parliament Act and any statutes scheduled to it, which would include the incorporation Act. (Other scheduled Acts might include the Habeas Corpus Acts, Magna Carta, the Race Relations Act, and the Sex Discrimination Act.) Thus, in relation to the new Parliament Act and to scheduled Acts, the Lords would have restored to it the absolute legislative veto which it enjoyed before 1911. Peers would have to be persuaded of the need to amend the new Bill of Rights (and other scheduled Acts), which, from time to time, they might be; on any occasions when they were not, they would be able to protect the existing law from encroachment. A variant on that might be centred on any new second chamber that might be created one day.[15] An elected second chamber might be given the power to delay legislation designed to amend the new Bill of Rights. That delay could last (if the second chamber desired it) for the whole life of a Parliament, thus providing the electorate with the chance to pass judgement at the following general election on the government which was proposing to derogate from fundamental rights. This could be said to amount to a redefinition of the ancient concept of the Queen in Parliament as a way round the orthodox view that legislation cannot be entrenched by the Queen in Parliament. The new second chamber would have to be based on a new constituent Act, which would define its powers and its relationship to the House of Commons, and which would abolish the House of Lords. The constituent Act would give the chamber an insurmountable legislative veto. The orthodox doctrine of parliamentary sovereignty would have to give way. For it would then be absurd to suggest that the House of Commons could ignore the new chamber's constituent Act and any veto imposed by that chamber of a Commons Bill, and seek to assert that that Bill had

---

[14] See 'Bill of Rights and Law Reform' in R. Holme and M. Elliott (eds.), *1688–1988: Time for a New Constitution* (London: Macmillan, 1988), 109–10.

[15] See Ch. 5.

become law despite the veto. To do so, the Commons would be relying on some mysterious, fundamental, and unalterable rule of parliamentary sovereignty which referred to a Parliament which by then would no longer exist in the form upon which that rule had been based.[16] That said, there would be two political difficulties inherent in such a scheme if it were put into being. It assumes a party in effective control of the second chamber which would be minded to oppose any Commons Bill which would derogate from the Bill of Rights. That would not necessarily be so. Obviously, whenever the *same* party was in control of both Houses, it would be unlikely that a veto would be used against the government—although as the House of Lords under the late Conservative Government showed us, that could not be taken for granted. Moreover, it is unlikely that a general election campaign could be fought on the single issue of a proposed amendment to the legislation on fundamental rights. Such simple things rarely happen in general elections, however much the political parties urge the voters to concentrate on one question. Despite those points, such a plan, if enacted, might tame the Leviathan of parliamentary sovereignty.

Lastly, there are judicial solutions to difficulties of entrenchment. Sir William Wade has argued that it is time the United Kingdom grew up and stopped mumbling feebly that nothing can be done to entrench legislation. His 'easy way out' would be to secure recognition of any entrenched provisions through a new judicial oath of office. An Act would discharge the judges from their existing oaths, and would require them to re-swear in terms obliging them to recognize and give effect to the terms of entrenched legislation (such as a new Bill of Rights).[17] Provided that the provision relating to the new oath was itself immunized against amendment, this would be a simple and effective means through which a Bill of Rights could be safeguarded. I would like to suggest a rather different approach to the judges. Their role in attempted entrenchment would be crucial, because in the end the law is what the judges say it is. So why do we not ask the judges, officially and formally, what their attitude

---

[16] See further on this point S. A. de Smith and R. Brazier, *Constitutional and Administrative Law*, 7th edn. (Harmondsworth: Penguin Books, 1994), 78–9.

[17] H. W. R. Wade, *Constitutional Fundamentals* (London: Stevens & Sons, 1989), ch. 3.

would be to legislation which purported to entrench itself? If the judiciary's reaction to purported entrenchment were known in advance, we could know whether to extend any further energy on such an enterprise. It is for the judges in the United Kingdom to say what they will recognize as valid and binding legislation. They invented the doctrine of parliamentary sovereignty; they have the power to curb their invention. Would they give effect to the entrenchment provisions of a new Bill of Rights (whether special parliamentary majorities, or a referendum, or any other means stipulated), so that amending or repealing legislation outside such mechanisms would be held to be of no effect? The question would be moot: their answer would be advisory only. The idea of putting such a question might be objected to as tending to prejudice judicial independence. I think that such an objection would be misconceived. Questions on the entrenchment point, put on behalf of the government (and ideally with the public support of the other party leaders as well), and answered on behalf of the whole senior judiciary, could not possibly interfere in any sense with the independence of the judges. If the notion of the government putting a question directly to the judges was considered to be an affront to the proprieties, the questioning might come from, say, the Select Committee on Home Affairs via the Lord Chancellor as head of the judiciary. To the extent that discreet soundings are already taken of the judges— before publication, for example, of major Criminal Justice Bills which would affect judicial sentencing powers—it is difficult to see what would be in the least offensive in putting *public* questions to them, or in publishing their answers. Public debate on the protection of fundamental freedoms would be enhanced greatly if this important and technical problem could be authoritatively answered by the only people whose attitude to it counts. Sometimes a direct, even though unusual, way through complex issues is the best route.

And so entrenchment may be exposed as a red herring in the debate about civil rights, trailed across the way of those wishing to map out a path towards further legislation. There are several ways of negotiating any obstacle caused by entrenchment. It might be— for who, other than the judges, can say?—that only a fairly weak form of entrenchment of rights would be possible in the United

Kingdom. Even if that proved to be so, however, that should not mean, in my opinion, that all further discussion of fresh statutory rights would be a futile exercise. On the other hand, it might be that greater protection of rights would be possible, through the device of seeking to redefine the Queen in Parliament. Entrenchment should not be the beginning and end of the Bill of Rights debate.

Parliamentary sovereignty has become more complete than the divine right of kings, and elective dictatorship has given governments supreme authority in the constitutional system. Those facts would not be so important if the electoral system did not grant uninhibited legislative power to Ministers who are returned by a minority of voters. Our constitutional laws, including those designed to secure basic civil rights, are not specially protected, and any government can limit individual freedom more or less as it wishes. Such a basis for a constitution is at best unsatisfactory and at worst offensive. The law on certain basic rights, such as the rights to life, liberty, property, free speech, and worship, ought to place awkward political and legal difficulties in the way of a House of Commons which wished to limit them—even if it were elected through a more representative method than at present. The current law on human rights is not satisfactory. The frequent reverses at Strasbourg, and the wide-ranging schemes of two of the political parties to bring about radical improvements, are indicators that all is far from well in the state of civil liberties in Britain. Such are the themes which point strongly towards the need further to enhance liberty.

But what is the case for continuing the British tradition of safeguarding rights through the courts and Parliament, thus eschewing the adoption of a new Bill of Rights? Some arguments should be dismissed with derision, or possibly with contempt. We are assured (especially by Conservatives) that individual rights in the United Kingdom are already adequately protected, and that, to the extent that adjustments prove to be necessary, ad hoc legislation can be passed for the purpose. Now, while the British do unquestionably enjoy better rights than citizens in several other countries, assertions such as these fly in the face of the evidence, evidence which two major political parties have accepted as proving the case for major changes in the law. Then we are told that a formal declaration of rights would be contrary to British tradition. So it would: but so what? And we are threatened with a flood of litigation if a Bill of Rights were adopted. This is no more than the old floodgates argument which is resurrected, usually in desperation, by many who oppose some change or other in the law. There is more food for thought in other strands of argument. The first runs that a Bill of Rights which is entrenched (whether as a matter of law or through its own moral force) is undemocratic, for it can prevent a government implementing parts of the programme which had been approved by the electorate. For example, a future government might wish to legislate further on abortion, but might be prevented from doing so in the manner it had indicated at the general election by the terms of the Bill of Rights. This argument becomes stronger the older any Bill might be, and the more representative the House of Commons might become, for Parliament would then be thwarted by tablets of stone carved by long-dead legislators. Another strand queries whether any Bill of Rights could, or even should, achieve finality. The meaning of legislation can only be definitively divined by judges who, in doing so, establish precedents. But what of awkward precedents established on a Bill of Rights? The courts might, for example, uphold legislation as being compatible with an exception in the Bill. The Opposition might view that as an indefensible use of such an exception. When they were next in power, should they put things right by securing an amendment to the Bill of Rights? If they cannot satisfy any amendment requirements, the Bill is undemocratic in the sense just indicated; if they *can* obtain an amendment, the value of having a measure whose purpose was supposed to be to secure rights indefinitely might be doubted.

That is not really an argument against judicial power as much as an argument that a draft Bill of Rights is strengthened if it has wide, and preferably cross-party, support, and conversely is weakened if it does not. But obviously there are arguments against judicial power in the protection of rights. The track-record of British judges in securing appropriate civil rights through the medium of the common law being unimpressive, it might be feared than in interpreting a Bill of Rights the judges might be too quick to find in favour of state power to the detriment of individual liberty. If a new Bill of Rights were (for whatever reason) difficult to amend, the role of the judiciary would clearly be the more important. As against that, two points may be made. First, British judges do have some experience of applying Bills of Rights. The Judicial Committee of the Privy Council has been the final imperial court of appeal since 1833, and has remained the supreme court for several independent Commonwealth countries. In that capacity the Judicial Committee has had to apply Commonwealth Bills of Rights. In the last fifteen years or so the Judicial Committee has tended to a more purposive and generous interpretation of such Bills, rather than a literal and restrictive one. The membership of the Judicial Committee and of the Appellate Committee of the House of Lords is much the same, and so the supreme court within the British legal system has had significant (even though indirect) experience in interpreting and applying Bills of Rights. Judges of all ranks have had to consider the terms of a Bill of Rights by having to become used to the provisions of the European Convention on Human Rights. Exposure to a new British Bill of Rights would not be quite the cultural shock which some suggest. The second point is that we do not have to assume that, in a process of constitutional change, the judiciary itself, and the structure of the courts in which they do justice, will remain the same. I will have more to say about that in the next chapter.

## The Next Steps

It will come as no surprise to the reader who has persevered thus far to learn that I believe the best way forward in the debate on civil rights would be for a wide-ranging review to be conducted of the most appropriate method for improving Britons' rights, even though the Human Rights Bill will undoubtedly improve matters. And the reader will expect me to say (as I do) that such a review would most appropriately be carried out by a body such as the Constitutional Commission proposed in Chapter 2, advised by an expert legal committee appointed by the Commission. No such study has so far been conducted, except for the very useful investigation by the House of Lords Select Committee on a Bill of Rights. The political debate on a possible Bill of Rights has revolved around the 'impossibility' of entrenchment, and the inability of the judges (who, in the process, would become politicized) to implement its provisions impartially. A rational investigation into the underlying issues, including of course a full examination of the desirability and possible means of specially protecting any new Bill, ought to be the necessary precursor of any political decision on whether to seek new arrangements for safeguarding human rights in the United Kingdom. Such an investigation (assuming that, by then, the European Convention will be part of municipal law) might recommend anything from a range of possibilities—to continue the status quo, or to suggest that a brand-new Bill of Rights be written. There would certainly be difficulties in trying to draft a brand-new Bill of Rights, particularly if it were designed to attract multi-party support. If the parties were to start with a blank sheet of paper, controversy would rage over many possible provisions—those on the method of voting which would be necessary to give effect to a right to fair elections, the right to property, to private health care and to private education, rights about trade union membership (to join or not to join, those are *both* the questions), and all the rest. In the meantime, there is much to commend the incorporation of the European Convention. Britain is bound by the European Convention in any event; the European Convention is enforced by the European Commission of Human Rights and the European Court; the British government always acquiesces in their findings; and there is no prospect of, or desire to, withdraw from the Convention. Quite apart from any other consideration, it ought to be politically attractive to place the terms of the Convention into a British statute, and require that its provisions be applied in all courts in the United Kingdom. When that is done under the current Human Rights Bill, enforcement would no longer be entirely a matter for a *European* court and judicial system. Condemnations from abroad should then be a thing of the past. The law would, once again, be in the hands of British judges. Such a change would also cut costs, because the delay in getting a ruling from the European Court (which can be as long as five years or even more) would be avoided, and the inevitable expense to litigants would be reduced. Such arguments ought to appeal to the chauvinism which still exists in parts of the Conservative and Labour Parties towards Europe, but for all that they represent perfectly sensible selling-points which, when adopted, would improve the lot of British citizens by making it much easier for them to enforce their rights.

But such incorporation would not, in my opinion, be enough. The European Convention is showing signs of the times in which it was written, particularly in the things which it does not seek to safeguard—rights to private property, succession rights, compensation for compulsory acquisition, and the freedom not to join a trade union. An ideal combination, therefore, would be to incorporate the Convention and to pass other specific legislation so as to protect rights that would otherwise be outside its ambit. How might all this be specially protected against the deprivations of elective dictatorship (assuming that that form of government were to continue)? If the judiciary were to indicate, in reply to my questions suggested earlier, that parliamentary sovereignty is parliamentary sovereignty, was, is, and will be, then I would find the most appealing of all the ways of giving some measure of protection to be a combination of both the interpretative method and a House of Lords veto. So, an Act incorporating the European Convention (and any other Acts setting out additional rights) would require that prior inconsistent legislation be of no effect, and that later legislation be interpreted in a way consistent with those Acts, unless that were impossible or unless the later legislation expressly stated that it was to override the Bill of Rights Act. The Parliament Acts 1911 and 1949 could be amended so as to restore to the House of Lords an absolute veto over any Bill which would amend or repeal anything in the Bill of Rights Act and any Acts forming part of it. The cussedness which the House of Lords has demonstrated over recent decades towards legislation of both parties might mean that there would be no guarantee of Lords consent to derogating legislation, even if proposed by a Conservative government. Such a mechanism would be completely consistent with even the most orthodox view of parliamentary sovereignty, but would provide a better check than could be imposed through the existing law. Of course, a government which was determined to amend a Bill of Rights Act *despite* a House of Lords veto could amend the Parliament Acts yet again to remove the newly restored veto, and could force such a Bill through under the Parliament Act itself (that is, after a Lords' delay of about a year). In doing so, the determination of that government to derogate from civil rights would appear the more stark. If recruitment to the House of Lords were to be improved in the ways indicated in Chapter 5, the existence of a veto against amending a Bill of Rights Act might prove the more efficacious, because in time that House would contain more independent peers. Convincing appeals to reason, rather than to the loyalties of party, would then be necessary if the Bill of Rights Act were to be amended with peers' consent.

Even if the United Kingdom were to adopt some form of Bill of Rights as part of its municipal law, a difficulty would remain: the judges. How could Parliament enact such a Bill and be reasonably sure that the judiciary would interpret and apply it broadly as Parliament wished? How, in particular, could Parliament be satisfied that its provisions would be applied impartially, without bias for or against any group, class, or interest? Questions about rights, or balancing one set of rights against a competing right or set of rights, occasionally requires judges to be sensitive to political issues. Are the judges currently able to carry out such balancing exercises in an acceptable way? Such questions raise wider issues about the composition of the judiciary, which I want to address in the next chapter.

# 9 Government, Law, and Judges

## Ministers, the Constitution, and the Law

THE United Kingdom does not have a Minister entirely responsible for constitutional affairs. As is so often the case, ad-hockery reigns: whenever a government decides to embark on a constitutional change it makes ministerial dispositions especially for the purpose, and winds them up when that purpose has been achieved (or has failed). Negotiations in the early 1970s to join the European Community? Let the Chancellor of the Duchy of Lancaster conduct them, under the supervision of the Foreign Secretary. Devolution of power to Scotland and Wales in the late 1970s? Let the Lord President of the Council be in charge, working in a newly created Constitution Unit in the Cabinet Office. The political parties are quite happy to go on in the same way in the future. The Labour Government that took office in 1997 did so committed to a bigger programme of constitutional reform than any previous government.[1] But this work was not entrusted to a single government department which might possess the expertise and resources which such grand schemes deserve. Rather, the programme was coordinated by a Cabinet Committee on Constitutional Reform Policy, chaired by the Prime Minister, and there was also another Cabinet Committee on devolution, and a Ministerial Subcommittee on the incorporation of the European Convention on Human Rights. A Constitution Secretariat in the Cabinet Office was charged with giving help to the various government departments involved. This approach was, of course, typical of what had gone before. The wide-ranging plans of the Liberal Democrats to work towards a written constitution, to introduce proportional representation, to create a Senate in place of

---

[1] See Ch. 3.

the House of Lords, and to adopt a Bill of Rights, would not, apparently, be spearheaded by new constitutional machinery, either. A contributory, although by no means dominant, factor in the United Kingdom's historical failure to reform its constitutional system may well have been the absence of adequate government machinery which could act as a focal point for ideas, as a catalyst for change, and as a depository of legislative and administrative expertise.[2] The Conservative Party can easily defend its refusal to allocate governmental resources appropriate to the importance of constitutional affairs on the ground that it rejects the case for general constitutional reform.[3] The other political parties have no such defence.

Governments of all colours, however, have had to make ministerial dispositions in relation to the general law. No government could claim or would wish to claim that it had no responsibility for legal affairs. Whether governments like it or not, important constitutional issues are entwined in that responsibility. They include the independence of the judges, the appropriate training for the judiciary which would not improperly interfere with that independence, ministerial accountability for the law, the administration of justice, and the provision of appropriate legal services for citizens. Yet the ministerial dispositions which have developed, mainly as between the Lord Chancellor and the Home Secretary, are such as would not be acceptable in other broadly similar states. No modern state which wished to establish ministerial responsibility for such things as the administration of justice, public order, the treatment of offenders, law reform, and the appointment of the judiciary would follow the British pattern and allocate those and related matters almost haphazardly between two Ministers. Nor would it place each of those Ministers in different chambers of the legislature, with one Minister (equivalent to the Lord Chancellor) having for good measure judicial and parliamentary duties as well. Such a state would not charge one of the Ministers (the equivalent of the Home Secretary) with two largely incompatible functions, police and public order on the one hand, and the protection of civil rights on the other. Nor would it

---

[2] These organizational questions are examined in depth in Constitution Unit, *Delivering Constitutional Reform* (London, 1996).

[3] See Ch. 1.

be likely to follow the United Kingdom in giving law responsibilities to another five Ministers as well.[4]

Under this chaotic British system the Lord Chancellor is responsible for judicial service matters (that is, judicial appointments, the determination of judicial salaries, and the disciplining of the lower judiciary); judicial administration; the state of the civil law, and legal aid and advice. If that were not enough for any Minister, he can also write chronicles of wasted time while acting as Speaker of the House of Lords—wasted time given that peers keep themselves in order and given that he is only occasionally present for business in which he has any departmental responsibility. The Lord Chancellor may also sit as a judge in the House of Lords. In all this the Lord Chancellor did not even have a junior Minister to help him until a Parliamentary Secretary was appointed in 1992.[5] That development brought the Lord Chancellor's Department (LCD) within the reach of the House of Commons for the first time, and the Select Committee on Home Affairs was also given oversight of the LCD (although—rightly—not of particular court cases or judicial appointments). In his turn, the Home Secretary is required to reconcile two inconsistent responsibilities: those relating to civil rights and justice (criminal-law reform, magistrates' courts, race relations legislation, data protection, nationality, and the like), and those concerning public order and security (the police, the Special Branch, MI5, and the treatment of offenders). It must be assumed that Home Secretaries can cope with this rather schizophrenic life, or else many would have left office very precipitately. But that is not the point. It is obvious that a Minister with vital public order responsibilities may be unable or unwilling to give enough of his energies to issues such as the freedom of the individual or minority rights. Indeed, his government's commitment to 'law and order' policies might mean that he would have no personal political incentive to argue for the enlargement and development of civil rights.

---

[4] The Prime Minister, the Attorney-General, the Solicitor-General, the Chancellor of the Duchy of Lancaster, and the Financial Secretary to the Treasury all have responsibilities for aspects of the law.

[5] The Attorney-General and the Solicitor-General are in no sense junior Ministers to the Lord Chancellor.

Highly undesirable results flow from a further division of responsibilities between the Home Office and the LCD. Because the Home Office is in charge of criminal law reform while the LCD is responsible for the state of the civil law, no single Minister has overall responsibility for law reform. If a particular proposed reform concerns the civil law (which quantitatively most will), pressure cannot be put by Members of Parliament directly on the Lord Chancellor to accept the need for that reform. Each government department is fully responsible for promoting changes in the law within its particular field, so that, for example, the Department for Education and Employment oversees trade union and employment law. Such devolution of law reform duties to individual departments is necessary and probably inevitable, given that expertise in particular areas of government is naturally concentrated in them; but departmental Ministers have many other calls on their time, and what is lacking is a single Minister who could spur ministerial colleagues to action. In establishing the political priorities for government legislation, inter-departmental claims for resources and parliamentary time are, in short, settled with insufficient ministerial weight behind the case for law reform. Further confusion in law reform responsibilities is caused by the pattern of reform bodies. The Criminal Law Revision Committee reports (when it reports at all) to the Home Secretary, and the Law Commission to the Lord Chancellor: but the Law Commission has also undertaken important criminal law work—especially in relation to work on a draft Criminal Code—for which the Lord Chancellor has no direct responsibility.

These ministerial dispositions have resulted in a complete lack of ministerial responsibility and accountability in a number of areas. The worst example concerns accountability to Parliament for judicial service matters. Lord Hailsham of St Marylebone LC frequently claimed that he was answerable to Parliament for such questions. He often proclaimed the virtue of his position, which interposed the Lord Chancellor between the independence of the judiciary and what he considered were improper attacks by Members of Parliament on the judges. That claim of accountability is really bogus—or at any rate is one whose truth has not been tested. From first to last during his Chancellorship no peer called Lord Hailsham to account in these matters. There were no questions or debate in that House either about the policy behind or the applications of his power to make judicial appointments, or his refusal to renew temporary judicial posts, or the removal from office of a Circuit judge in 1983. There were many opportunities for peers to inquire into these matters during, for example, the passage of legislation bearing on the administration of justice. Had the Lord Chancellor been in the House of Commons he would certainly have been challenged on such questions. In practice no Minister is now accountable for judicial service issues. As I will argue later, some of those matters should not be within any ministerial portfolio, but it is unsatisfactory to achieve that result in practice while none the less claiming that such ministerial responsibility does actually exist.

Some of the issues touched on so far concern technical legal matters. Others are of significant constitutional importance. The law and the constitution are inseparably mixed. The way in which a government equips itself to address such interlocking legal and constitutional issues is something which should attract the attention of constitutional reformers. One political party, the Liberal Democrats, does have plans to recast ministerial responsibility for the law: another, the Labour Party, had such plans, but alas ditched them before coming to power in 1997. The Liberal Democrats propose the creation of a Ministry of Justice.[6] It would be charged with the protection of human rights, the administration of the legal system, and law reform. The Home Office would retain its 'internal security' functions. It is not clear from the plan whether such a new Minister would sit in the House of Commons: proper accountability would require that he do so, but an earlier paper suggested that the Lord Chancellor might be the Minister of Justice, and that as such he should be enabled to sit in either House.[7] That cannot be right. Nor is it clear whether the new Minister would take responsibility for all law reform. Again, the earlier paper suggested just that, but a degree of devolution of responsibility to individual departments for law reform is unavoidable. But the general idea behind the plan—to

---

[6] See *Here We Stand: Proposals for Modernising Britain's Democracy*, Liberal Democrat Federal White Paper No. 6 (London, 1993), 48–9.

[7] *Government, Justice and Law*, Alliance Paper No. 1 (London, 1985).

rationalize ministerial tasks—is highly desirable. Labour had plans to abolish the Lord Chancellor's ministerial functions,[8] but abandoned them in 1995.[9] Under its former scheme a Minister of Legal Administration, sitting in the Commons, would have become responsible for all courts and tribunals, court procedure, the organization, training, and appointment of the legal professions, magistracy, and (indirectly) the judiciary, and for legal aid. The Home Secretary would have retained his duties with regard to the police, prisons, penal policy, and the criminal law. The Party deserved credit for abandoning its provisional, and in my opinion highly unwise, view that the Home Office and the LCD should be merged under one Minister, although I do not see what advantage would have been served in retaining a remaindered Lord Chancellor. Mr Tony Blair as Prime Minister continued the traditional arrangements for the Lord Chancellor and his Department, and for the Home Office. Once again the Conservative Party has nothing to contribute to the debate. The late Conservative Government was unconvinced by any of the proposals that had been made for new ministerial arrangements for the law.[10]

I want to set out a number of principles upon which reorganization of government in this area should be based. First, ministerial responsibility for the law should be fully founded in the House of Commons, and be subject to select committee scrutiny, in the same way as any other government activity. Secondly, ministerial dispositions should be related entirely to functions and efficiency, so that, for example, one department (the Home Office) should be responsible for matters such as public order and the treatment of offenders, while another department should be charged with responsibilities such as civil rights, constitutional development, the general oversight of the law and law reform, and judicial administration. Thirdly, any major recasting of ministerial responsibilities should take advantage of a fresh start, so that rather than trying to reform the office of Lord Chancellor, and trying to graft new and dynamic duties on to the

---

[8] See *Meet the Challenge: Make the Change* (London: Labour Party, 1989), 61.

[9] See *Access to Justice* (London: Labour Party, 1995), 7. See further Ch. 3.

[10] See, e.g. the Chancellor of the Duchy of Lancaster at 254 HC Debs. 2 (written answers 6 Feb. 1995).

LCD, a new department should be created and both the office of Lord Chancellor and the LCD should be abolished. Fourthly, judicial service matters (relating principally to judicial appointments, promotions and discipline) should be moved completely away from ministerial authority, and machinery independent of Ministers should be created to discharge responsibilities for them.

How might such principles be translated into practice?[11] At the centre of the reorganized machinery of government, I believe, should be a new Department of Law. Nomenclature is important, if only because some of the reaction against the proposals of the Haldane Committee on the Machinery of Government[12] over eighty years ago was fuelled by the use of the continental title of 'Ministry of Justice'. To avoid stirring up misplaced fears that a new government department would be intended to interfere in the judicial process, the word 'justice' would be better avoided. Rather, the work of the Department would be accurately summed up in the word 'law'. The principal duties of the Department might include the following: (*a*) civil rights, legal services, legal aid, and relations with the professions; (*b*) the reform of civil and criminal law (although the initial responsibility of other government departments for this would remain), and responsibility for all law reform agencies; (*c*) constitutional development, including responsibility for my suggested Constitutional Commission; (*d*) the provision, administration, and procedure of all courts and tribunals; and (*e*) determination of judicial salaries. If the Department of Law had duties such as those, the Home Office would be left with functions relating to public order, public safety, national security, the treatment of offenders and penal policy, the enforcement of immigration control, elections, broadcasting, and many minor, miscellaneous matters. Those are important responsibilities, most of which fit logically within a department such as the Home Office. The Home Secretary's main burden would involve fighting for the public money and parliamentary time necessary to fulfil those functions, without (as now) having to seek such money and time for different, and sometimes opposing, responsibilities as well.

[11] More detail is given in my article 'Government and the Law: Ministerial Responsibility for Legal Affairs' [1989] *Public Law* 64.

[12] *Report of the Committee on the Machinery of Government*, Cd. 9230 (1918), ch. x.

Some parts of such a settlement of duties within the proposed Department of Law would be politically more divisive than others, for they would go beyond a logical and efficient restructuring of ministerial responsibilities. Thus, for instance, there is a case for the new Secretary of State for Law having as an important statutory duty the establishment and maintenance of comprehensive legal services, perhaps by analogy with the duty of the Secretary of State for Health to promote a comprehensive National Health Service. Whether such a duty were accorded to the Law Secretary, and what its precise nature would be, would in large part depend on the political colour of the government which set up the Department. Such a duty would undoubtedly be rejected by the Conservatives, who would also probably not agree to the Law Secretary having responsibility for the whole civil rights field. But the new Department's role in such matters could be conventional and permissive, rather than statutory and directory, so that a Conservative Minister and Cabinet would be able to take the view that fresh protection of human rights was not warranted, or that resources did not permit major extensions in legal services, whereas a non-Conservative administration might come to the opposite view. Depending on the Law Secretary's determination and clout in a non-Conservative government, he might push such matters forward in ways that would be difficult to imagine within the present structures of the LCD or the Home Office. For the first time, one department could be responsible for civil rights questions without additionally having (as the Home Office has now) duties to preserve national security and public order, to prevent crime, and to support the police. For the first time, the appropriate content of important laws could be considered ministerially as much from a civil liberties point of view as any other, and could be fought for interdepartmentally (especially, perhaps, against the Home Office), in Cabinet committees, in the Cabinet, and in Parliament.

If a Constitutional Commission along the lines advocated in this book were to be set up,[13] a Minister would have to be responsible for obtaining the public money required for the Commission's premises, staff, research work, and so on. A Minister would also have

---

[13] See Ch. 2.

to negotiate from time to time with the other political parties about certain references to the Commission, and would have to take charge of Bills emanating from the Commission. The new Department of Law could sensibly have a constitutional affairs division within it. If it did, there would be at long last within the government a permanent and central ministerial unit charged with constitutional development.

It is impossible to justify the present split of responsibilities between the Home Office and the LCD for the state of the criminal and civil law, and for their reform. The Department of Law would be responsible for both—but in a way which would maintain the necessary diffusion of some responsibility to individual government departments. The Law Secretary alone would decide on the importance of particular law reform measures, and would have to argue for parliamentary time in which to enact them. A watching brief would also be kept by the Law Secretary over the fate of reform proposals emanating from bodies such as departmental committees of inquiry, set up by other Ministers and reporting to them. The Department of Law would not, however, attempt to take over the law reform which is now undertaken by individual government departments: no one central department could match the knowledge and policy expertise which exists in those departments. The Department of Law would not be involved in criminal law enforcement, which would remain with the Home Office; but the Department would take over responsibility for the state of the criminal law. This law reform work would shade into the new Department's general oversight of the form of legislation sponsored by other departments, and into its responsibility for the consolidation programme. One purpose behind giving the Department that oversight would be simple: to ensure that new legislation was as comprehensible as possible. All government legislation would be tested for comprehensibility and other desirable qualities in the Department of Law, which would have the last word over the form in which it was submitted to Parliament. The Lord Chancellor and the Law Officers would cease to have a role in such work, and the Cabinet Legislation Committee's notional function of watching over the form of legislation could formally cease. As an overall consequence the quality of such legislation ought to improve.

The only function of the Law Secretary which would impinge directly and personally on the judiciary would be the determination of their salaries (with the consent of the Prime Minister as Minister for the Civil Service), a duty currently conferred by statute on the Lord Chancellor. In the ways in which those salaries are now set and increased, however (being charged on Consolidated Fund Services, with the recommendations of the Senior Salaries Review Body normally being implemented by Ministers), that task in practice has no effect on judicial independence and may be safely entrusted to Ministers.

The Law Secretary would, of course, be a Member of Parliament, and he should have ministerial support appropriate to the size of his departmental duties, including one or two junior Ministers. There is no cogent reason why the Law Secretary should necessarily be a lawyer. Ministers are not expected to be professionals in their departmental specialities, and the Law Secretary would be no exception. Parliamentary supervision of the two Ministers who would have responsibility for legal affairs under this scheme, the Home Secretary and the Law Secretary, would be asserted through the House of Commons. A Select Committee on the Department of Law would be established, and no part of the Department's duties would be beyond its reach.

## The Judges

The judges play a pivotal part in the British constitution. It is misconceived to propose major reforms to that constitution, many of which would require changes in the law, without addressing the general question of the judiciary. I want to turn to that question now.

Any suggestion of major reorganization of ministerial responsibility for the law is usually met with the objection that the judges would become subject to ministerial control and dependent on ministerial approval for appointment and promotion. 'Judicial independence' is a phrase which has often been deployed in order to maintain the status quo. Lord Chancellors have vigorously asserted that judicial independence requires a continuance of the present arrangements.

Lord Hailsham asserted this the most vigorously and his successors have done nothing to dissociate themselves from that view. What does judicial independence, properly defined, entail? In general, the public must feel confident in the integrity and impartiality of the judiciary: judges must therefore be secure from undue influence and be autonomous in their own field. That possibly implies that neither the government nor Parliament should have any role in the appointment or removal of judges, which has never been the case in this country. More precisely, judicial independence may be said to require: (*a*) that appointments to judicial office, renewal of part-time appointments, and promotions, should not depend on uncontrolled ministerial patronage; (*b*) that judges should be free from improper attempts by Ministers, Members of Parliament, or peers to influence the result of cases still under adjudication; (*c*) that judicial salaries should not be reduced; and (*d*) that judges should not be removed from office unfairly or without reason. Those four precepts should be the bedrock of judicial independence and should find broad acceptance in any western liberal democracy. While the existing machinery of government and parliamentary rules are generally compatible with the second, third and fourth of those precepts, the first is not satisfied at all.

The entire judiciary in England and Wales owes its appointment to one, and occasionally to two, politicians. Anyone wishing to become a judge, however low or however high, must first receive the approval of the Lord Chancellor. Even those aspiring to the highest judicial offices, in the Court of Appeal and the House of Lords, to which appointment is made by the Queen on the Prime Minister's recommendation, must in practice have the Lord Chancellor's support. He is always consulted by the Prime Minister on such appointments, and it would be most unlikely today that someone would be recommended against his wishes.[14] Moreover, since 1980 a career structure has been developed so that no one is appointed to a full-time judicial office without first having proved himself to be up to the mark in a relevant part-time post to which appointment is made

---

[14] Indeed, the Select Committee on Home Affairs has recommended that the Prime Minister's formal role in judicial appointments could be ended: 3rd Report from the Home Affairs Committee, *Judicial Appointments Procedures*, HC 52 (1995–6), i, para. 128.

by the Lord Chancellor. No one will be appointed to the High Court without such a successful apprenticeship. Appointments to the Court of Appeal and to the judicial House of Lords are nowadays made exclusively from the High Court, so that the career progression runs from appointment to part-time judicial work, to appointment to the High Court, and beyond. The Lord Chancellor's patronage is thus all-pervasive throughout the judiciary.[15]

Obviously the longer a Prime Minister and Lord Chancellor hold office the more judicial appointments will fall to be made. So Mrs Thatcher and her Lord Chancellors between them appointed all the current Lords of Appeal in Ordinary, all the Lords Justices of Appeal, and three-quarters of the High Court bench. Such ministerial patronage may reasonably cause concern about the precise role of Ministers—for the Lord Chancellor's judicial and parliamentary duties must not obscure the simple fact that he is as much a departmental Minister as any other member of the Cabinet. Indeed, some of the criticisms voiced in the past about a possible Minister of Justice (lawyers' dependence on a party politician for preferment, and so on) could in fact be more appropriately aimed at the Lord Chancellor himself. His role in judicial appointments may be objected to on a number of grounds. First, the concentration of power in the hands of one person, without the benefit of a structured system of advice, is unsatisfactory. The patronage system at the disposal of Lord Chancellors, to put it bluntly, looks bad. Secondly, the increasing size of both branches of the profession means that the civil servants in the LCD cannot have adequate knowledge of all potential candidates for judicial posts or of the particular situation in each of the six Circuits. This problem will worsen as more solicitors are considered for senior judicial appointments under the Courts and Legal Services Act 1990. Despite the soundings taken from the LCD, the appointments system is too centralized. Lastly, it is notorious that the present system produces few women and ethnic-minority judges. In late 1995 all the Lords of Appeal were men, there was only one Lady Justice of Appeal, and seven women High Court judges (alongside eighty-nine male colleagues); some 15 per cent of

---

[15] The new qualifications for judicial appointment contained in the Courts and Legal Services Act 1990 will not alter this career progression or ministerial patronage.

Recorders and Assistant Recorders were female. Five Circuit judges (out of 517) and twelve Recorders (out of 891) were of ethnic-minority origin.[16] Those figures are depressing, especially given that junior judicial posts constitute the bottom rung of the career progression to the top judicial jobs. There may, of course, be reasons why this is not entirely the fault of the appointments system: if, for example, there is prejudice in the profession against black people, fewer will be able to enter or stay in it and the pool of potential judges will be smaller. But a different appointments system might bring with it greater enthusiasm to seek out qualified people from groups which are now absurdly under-represented on the bench. Now the last Conservative Lord Chancellor, Lord Mackay of Clashfern, adopted a comprehensive equal opportunities policy designed to increase the appointment of suitably qualified women and ethnic-minority judges,[17] and that policy is being continued by Lord Irvine of Lairg LC. It is too early to assess the impact that that policy is having on the problem.

The other three components of judicial independence noted earlier are (with one proviso) achieved through the present arrangements. That proviso concerns the tenure position of the lower judiciary, which is conspicuously weak. They are subject to non-renewal of part-time appointments, and to removal, at the hand of the Lord Chancellor, advised by his officials. This is a disturbing accretion of power in a Minister's hands, can be controversial in its use, and may not always be exercised incontrovertibly within the requirements of natural justice. Even Lord Hailsham acknowledged that the Lord Chancellor's disciplinary power was unsatisfactory and accepted the principle of a judicial complaints board which could hear complaints and advise the Lord Chancellor.

The machinery of government which concerns the law does not have to be maintained in its present form in order to protect the essentials of judicial independence. On the contrary, reform of that machinery is needed so as to remove the theoretical threat which is posed to it by ministerial power in judicial service matters. Indeed, the Liberal Democrats want to set up a Judicial Service Commission

---

[16] See 3rd Report from the Home Affairs Committee, paras. 77, 92.
[17] See 555 HL Debs. *28–29* (written answers 23 May 1994).

which would nominate all the senior judges to office, and consisting of a President, five judges, four barristers or advocates, four solicitors, and four lay members.[18] The Party does not appear to have addressed the question of how judges of Circuit rank and below should be appointed, a matter which is of at least equal importance given the career structure within the judiciary, and the large numbers of such appointments that have to be made. In Opposition, Labour wished to establish an independent commission, responsible to the Lord Chancellor, to recommend the appointment of judges.[19] The precise relationship between that commission and the Lord Chancellor would clearly be of great constitutional significance. An improved appointments system for magistrates, designed to ensure that benches reflected the communities which they served, would also be put in place. In 1997 a consultation paper was promised from the new Labour Lord Chancellor inviting views on the desirability of setting up a judicial appointments commission, and on the practical consequences of doing so. But the Lord Chancellor later decided that other matters had to take priority, and any such paper would have to wait.

I would go rather further than the Liberal Democrats and the Labour Party. I believe that Britain needs both a Judicial Service Commission and Circuit Judicial Committees. If a Judicial Service Commission were to take responsibility for judicial service matters, a remarkable amount of ministerial patronage—inappropriate, surely, in the context of the separation of powers and the proper demands of judicial independence—would disappear. Once ministerial nomination and election are ruled out as acceptable methods of choosing judges, a mechanism based at least in part on judicial self-perpetuation is the only alternative. A statutory Judicial Service Commission could take over the roles of both the Prime Minister and the Lord Chancellor in appointing Lords of Appeal in Ordinary, Lords Justices of Appeal, High Court judges and the four heads of divisions. The composition of the Commission (as in many Commonwealth states) might be drawn predominantly from representatives of the Lords of Appeal,

---

[18] *Here We Stand: Proposals for Modernising Britain's Democracy*, Liberal Democrat Federal White Paper No. 6 (London, 1993), 49.

[19] *Access to Justice*, 12–14.

Lords Justices, and High Court judges, and would also include all the heads of divisions; the chairmanship might rotate among those heads. Some lay membership would be important, partly to help offset professional insularity, and partly to ensure that the case was argued for widening the pool of potential judicial candidates. The Commission could meet in consultation with senior officials of the Department of Law, whose views on, for example, any requests for additional judge-power could be weighed by the members of the Commission, and those officials might act as informal liaison with the Law Secretary. The Commission would also have its own civil service staff. In carrying out its appointment duties, the Commission would arrange for the soundings which are now conducted by the LCD as to suitable candidates for appointment. The duty of receiving, investigating, if possible resolving, and if necessary adjudicating upon complaints made against senior judges would also fall to the Commission. Such complaints are now largely dealt with informally by the Lord Chancellor or the Lord Chief Justice: sometimes they result in public reprimands or administrative action. Some (perhaps many) of the relatively few complaints now made would continue to be answered by advice to appeal; others would certainly be rejected; those which were accepted for adjudication by the Commission could be investigated on its behalf, perhaps by a senior silk. Probably (as now) an undertaking as to future conduct from the judge in question would often be enough. Any serious criticism of a senior judge by the Commission as a whole—criticism by his peers—would be taken very seriously by him; it might well result in resignation. The parliamentary address removal procedure could remain, to be activated in the unlikely event of a judge refusing to resign despite condemnation by the Commission. There would be no need to change the statutory tenure now enjoyed by these judges.

Such a Commission would not actually represent a very radical departure. Extensive consultations already take place between the Lord Chancellor and the heads of division about, for example, candidates for senior judicial office; the Commission would continue them. The system that now requires a potential High Court judge to do satisfactory part-time work as a Recorder, or as a Circuit or Deputy High Court judge, before appointment as a High Court judge, would remain, as would the present promotions system from the High Court to the Court of Appeal, and from the Court of Appeal to the House of Lords. As far as discipline is concerned, the informal interviews with judges about whom complaints have been lodged could be just as effective if carried out on behalf of a Judicial Service Commission. The overwhelming advantage of the creation of such a Commission would be, however, that doubts and fears engendered by ministerial patronage would be ended.[20]

It is important not to overlook the inadequacies of the system of appointments to the lower judiciary. I believe that those inadequacies would be largely corrected if a Circuit Judicial Committee were established in each of the six Circuits to advise the Judicial Service Commission on the appointment of acting stipendiary and stipendiary magistrates, Assistant Recorders, Recorders, and Circuit judges. The local advisory committees which now advise the Lord Chancellor on the appointment of lay magistrates could in future make their recommendations to the local Circuit Judicial Committee. The Circuit Judicial Committees could also have disciplinary authority over the lower judiciary, as well as the duty to decide on the renewal of Assistant Recorderships and Recorderships. An advantage of creating the Circuit Judicial Committee tier would be that the burden which would otherwise fall entirely on the Judicial Service Commission (and which might call into question whether its judicial members could cope with it as well as with their court work) would be greatly eased through being shared. Other advantages would be that advice to the Commission, based on conditions in the Circuits, would be formalized (unlike the Lord Chancellor's present soundings); that decisions to recommend appointments would be shared by a number of people representative of legitimate interests, acting locally; and that the present role of a Minister, the Lord Chancellor, as prosecutor, jury and judge in disciplinary matters would cease. Indeed, if a Law Secretary were appointed, with a rationalization of ministerial functions between him and the Home Secretary, together with the setting up of this Commission and the six Committees, the

---

[20] Nevertheless, the Select Committee on Home Affairs (dividing on party lines) rejected the case for a new commission; 3rd Report from the Home Affairs Committee, para. 142.

office of Lord Chancellor could be abolished along with the Lord Chancellor's Department.

Progress has been made in improving the quality of judicial work through the efforts of the Judicial Studies Board since 1979. The compulsory residential training courses for Assistant Recorders and Recorders, followed by periods sitting with an experienced judge before they may sit on their own, is better than nothing. Judicial training still has rather a long way to go. Why do newly appointed High Court judges not have to undergo compulsory refresher-training? Why are judges of the Court of Appeal and of the House of Lords immune from training? When major new statutes affecting the work of the courts are enacted, why is there no compulsory instruction in the new law? For far too long senior judges especially have been expected to do their best without such help, rather as if they were gifted amateurs. That state of affairs is sometimes justified once again by the lame excuse that such instruction would jeopardize judicial independence. But formal explanations to the judges of the policies and principles behind legislation would in no sense threaten their ability to apply the law in particular cases without fear or favour, affection or ill will. Moreover, the more radical is the legislative departure from traditional thinking, the greater becomes the need for judicial education.

## A New Supreme Court

England already has a Supreme Court, although I doubt whether many non-lawyers (and even some lawyers) know what it is. The Court of Appeal, the High Court, and the Crown Court all make up the Supreme Court—not for the United Kingdom, but for England and Wales only.[21] The jurisdiction of the judicial House of Lords would have been abolished in 1874, had not Mr Disraeli displaced Mr Gladstone in the nick of time. A retentionist movement gathered sufficient strength to ensure that, under the Appellate Jurisdiction Act 1876, the House of Lords remained at the apex of the judicial

---

[21] Supreme Court Act 1981, s. 1.

system, alongside the Judicial Committee of the Privy Council for imperial appeals. The title of Supreme Court was designated by the Liberal Government for the new Court of Appeal and High Court: when the judicial House of Lords was confirmed in 1876 it remained supreme in the hierarchy but was not included in that name.

There is a strong case for establishing a new Supreme Court, entirely separate from the legislative House of Lords. It is wrong in principle that senior judges are also legislators. This is not so much because the participation in debates by the Law Lords and other peers who are judges offends the principle of the separation of powers (although it certainly does that): rather, it is objectionable because interventions by the judges in the House of Lords occasionally put them in the front line of political controversy. Professor Griffith has catalogued those interventions.[22] Notable interventions in the last decade have included speeches during the debates on the government's Green Papers on the reform of the legal professions and on the Courts and Legal Services Bill in 1990. Six Lords of Appeal joined the debate on the Green Papers, along with the Lord Chief Justice and the Master of the Rolls. All were highly critical of the policies behind the changes: the language used to oppose government policy by the Master of the Rolls in particular was perhaps the most trenchant ever uttered by a serving judge. Senior judges in the House of Lords were also bitterly critical of the Conservative Government's criminal justice legislation, criticisms which often put the Home Secretary and (in particular) the Lord Chief Justice at public loggerheads. These interventions go way beyond any comfortable notion that Law Lords and other peer-judges merely assist the House on the technical details of legislation (although they do that as well). Given that these senior judges are able to communicate their views on policy questions directly to the government, through, for example, the Judges' Council, Ministers would still have the benefit of their advice if they were excluded from membership of the House of Lords. The House as a legislative body would lose highly experienced lawyers if that were done, but a sizeable percentage of other peers have legal qualifications. Any convention which might

[22] J. A. G. Griffith, *The Politics of the Judiciary*, 5th edn. (London: Fontana, 1997), 42–5.

have existed which kept peer-judges to uncontroversial, technical matters in the House of Lords has ceased to exist, and it is time that they ceased to sit in that House.

The simplest way to effect the creation of a new Supreme Court would be through the abolition of the judicial House of Lords, and by the transfer of its functions, together with those of the Judicial Committee of the Privy Council, to the new Supreme Court. If Commonwealth states which retain appeals to the Judicial Committee objected to that on the ground that the Judicial Committee is perceived as being a Commonwealth court set apart from the British court system, the Judicial Committee could be kept as a separate body for such appeals. So the new Supreme Court might have a Commonwealth jurisdiction; its United Kingdom jurisdiction might consist of two main elements. First, it could keep the civil jurisdiction now exercised by the House of Lords, but it should not succeed to that House's criminal jurisdiction. The decisions of the House of Lords in criminal appeals have had lamentable effects on criminal law which have often had to be corrected by legislation, and that jurisdiction should not be continued. Secondly, the new Supreme Court might also have a special part to play in constitutional matters. If a new, formal declaration of civil rights were enacted for the United Kingdom, a leapfrogging procedure might enable appeals based on it to go straight from the court of first instance to the Supreme Court. This would shorten proceedings, and would allow authoritative rulings to be given on civil rights questions. It could also be given jurisdiction over disputed questions about the powers of the Scottish Parliament, the Welsh Assembly, and any English regional assemblies. In that way, the Court would ensure that the constitutional balance between the nations and regions of the United Kingdom set by Parliament was maintained, and that the general civil and constitutional law in England, Scotland, Wales, and Northern Ireland was developed in a unified way.

Given the importance of this new Court and the political context of part of its proposed jurisdiction, I think it would be right that the members of the Court should be subject to a new selection procedure. The basic qualification might be the same as for a Lord of Appeal in Ordinary, but candidates could be named by the new

Judicial Service Commission, and could then be examined by a joint select committee of both Houses. Its task would be to satisfy itself that candidates were fit and proper people to be appointed to the apex of the legal system. Part of the inquiry would be directed to the political, philosophical, and social views and attitudes of candidates. If the Supreme Court had functions in relation to civil rights, the judges would necessarily have to adjudicate from time to time on controversial matters, and it would be important that candidates' views were publicly known and their acceptability tested. There is currently no mechanism in the United Kingdom through which suitability for high judicial office can be investigated in detail, and if necessary at length; there is no means through which the weaknesses of a British equivalent of Mr Robert Bork[23] could be brought out so as to bar his appointment. Traditionalist may well view this proposal with horror: what price judicial independence in such a scheme, with political interference in the judicial selection process? But it would have nothing to do with judicial independence, and of course once appointed Supreme Court judges would have a very high degree of security of tenure. Indeed, as some appointments to the United States Supreme Court have shown, attempts to make partisan appointments to uphold the philosophy of the appointing President have often backfired. There would be a political intervention in the appointment process, but in my opinion that would be an advantage if it fully brought out into the public domain the political and social beliefs and attitudes of those who would have such an important part in the governance of the United Kingdom. A Court which would hold sway in constitutional and civil rights issues must not be composed only of men, drawn from a small pool, unrepresentative of the general population.

A recasting of ministerial responsibility for the law and for constitutional affairs along the lines that I have suggested would result in a modern, functional, accountable, and efficient system. Far from being faced with new threats to their proper independence, judges would be more free from ministerial control than they are now. The remit of the House of Commons would be extended into areas of

---

[23] Mr Bork's nomination to the Supreme Court was rejected by the United States Senate on the grounds of his unsuitability.

ministerial responsibility which until now have been blocked off from democratic investigation. One government department would have permanent duties in relation to constitutional development. Taken with the suggested Constitutional Commission, the constitution and the law might, over time, be put into a better and more appropriate shape for the new millennium.

# Bibliography

*A Voice for Wales* (Cm. 3718 (1997) ).

BAGEHOT, W., *The English Constitution* (first pub. 1867; London: Fontana, 1963).

BELL, J., *French Constitutional Law* (Oxford: Clarendon Press, 1992).

BENN, T., *Arguments for Socialism* (London: Cape, 1979).

—— Commonwealth of Britain Bill (HC Bill 161 (1990–1) ).

BOGDANOR, V., *Multi-Party Politics and the Constitution* (Cambridge: Cambridge University Press, 1988).

—— *The Monarchy and the Constitution* (Oxford: Clarendon Press, 1995).

—— *The People and the Party System* (Cambridge: Cambridge University Press, 1981).

BRAZIER, R., *Constitutional Practice*, 2nd edn. (Oxford: Clarendon Press, 1994).

—— *Constitutional Texts* (Oxford: Clarendon Press, 1991).

—— 'Enacting a Constitution' [1992] *Statute Law Review* 104.

—— 'Government and the Law: Ministerial Responsibility for Legal Affairs' [1989] *Public Law* 64.

—— *Ministers of the Crown* (Oxford: Clarendon Press, 1997).

BUTLER, D., 'Electoral Reform', in J. Jowell and D. Oliver (eds.), *The Changing Constitution*, 3rd edn. (Oxford: Oxford University Press, 1994).

COMMITTEE ON STANDARDS IN PUBLIC LIFE, *First Report* (Cm. 2850 (1995) ).

CONSERVATIVE POLITICAL CENTRE, *The House of Lords: Report of the Review Committee* (London, 1978).

CONSTITUTIONAL COMMISSION, *Final Report* (Australian Government Printing Service, 1988).

CONSTITUTION UNIT, *Delivering Constitutional Reform* (London, 1996).

—— *Human Rights Legislation* (London, 1996).

—— *Reform of the House of Lords* (London, 1996).

CROSSMAN, R., *Diaries of a Cabinet Minister* (London: Cape, 1977).

DE SMITH, S. A., and BRAZIER, R., *Constitutional and Administrative Law*, 7th edn. (Harmondsworth: Penguin Books, 1994).

DICEY, A. V., *Introduction to the Study of the Law of the Constitution* (first pub. 1885; London: Macmillan, 1959).

DUMMETT, M., *Principles of Electoral Reform* (Oxford: Clarendon Press, 1997).

ELECTORAL REFORM SOCIETY and the CONSTITUTION UNIT, *Report of the Commission on the Conduct of Referendums* (1996).

EWING, K., and GEARTY, C., *Freedom under Thatcher: Civil Liberties in Modern Britain* (Oxford: Clarendon Press, 1990).

FINER, S. E., BOGDANOR, V., and RUDDEN, B., *Comparing Constitutions* (Oxford: Clarendon Press, 1995).

GANZ, G., *Understanding Public Law*, 2nd edn. (London: Fontana, 1994).

GORNIG, G., and RECKEWERTH, S., 'The Revision of the German Basic Law' [1997] *Public law* 137.

GRIFFITH, J. A. G., *The Politics of the Judiciary*, 5th edn. (London: Fontana, 1997).

HAILSHAM, LORD, *The Dilemma of Democracy: Diagnosis and Prescription* (London: Collins, 1978).

HASELER, S., *Britain's Ancien Régime* (London: Cape, 1991).

HANSARD SOCIETY, *Report of the Commission on Electoral Reform* (London, 1976).

HARLOW, C., 'Power from the People', in P. McAuslan and J. F. McEldowney (eds.), *Law, Legitimacy and the Constitution* (London: Sweet & Maxwell, 1985).

HEWART, LORD, *The New Despotism* (London: Ernest Benn, 1929).

HOLME, R., and ELLIOT, M. (eds.), *1688–1988: Time for a New Constitution* (London: Macmillan, 1988).

HOME AFFAIRS COMMITTEE, 3rd Report, *Judicial Appointments Procedures* (HC 52 (1995–6) ).

HOOD PHILLIPS, O., *Constitutional and Administrative Law*, 7th edn. (London: Sweet & Maxwell, 1987).

*House of Lords Reform* (Cmnd. 3799 (1968) ).

INSTITUTE FOR PUBLIC POLICY RESEARCH, *A Written Constitution for the United Kingdom* (London: Mansell, 1993).

JACONELLI, J., *Enacting a Bill of Rights: The Legal Problems* (Oxford: Clarendon Press, 1980).

JOWELL, J., and OLIVER, D., *The Changing Constitution*, 3rd edn. (Oxford: Clarendon Press, 1994).

LABOUR PARTY, *Access to Justice* (London, 1995).

—— *Meet the Challenge: Make the Change* (London, 1989).

—— *New Labour: Because Britain Deserves Better* (general election manifesto) (London, 1997).

—— *Report of the Working Party on Electoral Systems* (London, 1993).

LABOUR PARTY and the LIBERAL DEMOCRATS, *Report of the Joint Consultative Committee on Constitutional Reform* (London, 1997).

LAKEMAN, E., *How Democracies Vote* (London: Faber, 1970).

LIBERAL DEMOCRATS, *A Parliament for the People*, Policy Paper No. 20 (London, 1996).

—— *Here We Stand: Proposals for Modernizing Britain's Democracy*, Federal White Paper No. 6 (London, 1993).

—— *Make the Difference* (general election manifesto) (London, 1997).

MCAUSLAN, P., and MCELDOWNEY, J. F. (eds.), *Law, Legitimacy and the Constitution* (London: Sweet & Maxwell, 1985).

MCFADDEN, J., 'The Scottish Constitutional Convention' [1995] *Public Law* 215.

MACKINTOSH, J., *The British Cabinet* (London: Stevens & Sons, 1977).

MARSHALL, G., *Constitutional Conventions* (Oxford: Clarendon Press, 1984).

*Rights Brought Home: The Human Rights Bill* (Cm. 3782 (1997) ).

ROUSSEAU, J.-J., *Social Contract* (first pub. 1772), ed. G. D. H. Cole (London: Dent, 1973).

SAMPFORD, C., ' "Recognize and Declare": An Australian Experiment in Codifying Conventions' 7 (1987) *Oxford Journal of Legal Studies* 369.

*Scotland's Parliament* (Cm. 3658 (1997) ).

SCOTTISH CONSTITUTIONAL CONVENTION, *Scotland's Parliament: Scotland's Right* (Edinburgh, 1995).

SHELL, D., *The House of Lords* (Hemel Hempstead: Philip Allan, 1988).

SUNKIN, M., and PAYNE, S., *The Nature of the Crown* (Oxford: Clarendon Press, 1998).

WADE, H. W. R., *Constitutional Fundamentals* (London: Stevens & Sons, 1989).

# Index

abdication crisis 3
accountability:
    judiciary 166
    Lord Chancellor 165–6
    Members of Parliament 59, 72
    ministers 165–6
additional member system 75–6, 77
administration of justice 40
armed conflict 109, 122–3
Australian Constitution 26–30, 37
    alternative vote 80–1
    amendments 27
    Constitutional Commission 27–30;
        terms of reference 28–9
    constitutional conventions 27–8
    elections 80–1
    expert committees 30–1
    judiciary 29
    proportional representation 75

Bagehot, Walter 10
Benn, Tony 109
Bill of Rights 1–2, 12
    amendment 151–3, 158, 160
    civil rights 148–61
    drafting 158
    entrenchment 148–59
    European Convention on Human
        Rights 153
    House of Commons 151
    House of Lords 151, 153, 158–61
    interpretation 148, 152
    Joint Consultative Committee on
        Constitutional Reform 49, 50
    judiciary 148, 152, 154–5, 157–9,
        161
    Labour Government 39
    Labour Party 148–50

    legislation 153; compatibility with
        152; overriding 160
    Liberal Democrats 49, 147–8
    parliamentary sovereignty 150, 151
    Privy Council 158
    select committees 158–9
    UK Constitution 150–1
Blair, Tony 9–10, 41, 47, 64, 119,
    122
British Constitution see UK
    Constitution
budget 117–18
Burke, Edmund 58

cabinet 110–25
    armed conflict 122–3
    Blair, Tony 119, 122
    budget 117–18, 120
    Chancellor of the Exchequer
        117–18
    collective responsibility 8–9
    committees 118–20, 162
    Conservative Party 111
    decision-making 117–21
    economic policy 117–18, 120
    elections 111–12, 116–17, 121
    European Convention on Human
        Rights 162
    government 110–25
    Joint Consultative Cabinet
        Committee 19, 22, 53, 54
    judiciary 173
    Labour Government 111
    legislation 170
    Liberal Democrats 53
    Lord Chancellor 173
    Major, John 119, 122
    Parliament, dissolution of 116

cabinet (*cont.*):
  patronage 110–12
  Prime Minister 109, 110–25
  reform 162
  reshuffles 108, 110–12
  royal prerogative 120, 122
  safeguards 120, 122
  secrecy 117–19
  shadow 111, 120, 121
  sovereignty 123–4
  sub-cabinet decision-making
    118–19
  Thatcher, Margaret 116–17, 122
Callaghan, James 112, 121, 132
centralization 46
Chancellor of the Exchequer 117–18
Charter 88, 12
Charter of Rights 39, 41, 148
Church of England 99, 112, 113–14
Circuit Judicial Committees 175–6,
    177
civil rights:
  Bill of Rights 147–8, 150–61
  Charter of Rights 39, 41, 148
  Conservative Party 147, 169
  Constitutional Commission of the
    UK 158–9
  defending 144–61
  European Convention on Human
    Rights 145–50
  government 144–5, 148, 157
  Home Office 164
  House of Commons 156
  House of Lords 160–1
  judicial review 147
  judiciary 146–9, 157
  Labour Government 148–9
  Labour Party 148–50
  legislation 146–7, 149, 156
  Liberal Democrats 147–8
  ministers 146–7
  Parliament 148, 150, 156–7
  review 158–7
  sovereignty 150, 156

  Supreme Court 180–1
  Thatcher, Margaret 145
  UK Constitution 150
civil service 112, 114
coalitions 5–6
  Constitutional Commission for the
    UK 32–3
  democracy 78
  dissolution 136
  emergencies 138–9
  government 506, 32–3, 138–9
  Liberal Democrats 134–5
  Prime Minister 136–9
  proportional representation 78
  Queen 134, 136
committees of inquiry 17, 23
Conservative Party *see also* Thatcher,
    Margaret
  cabinet 111
  civil rights 147, 169
  constitutions 5
  elections 63, 64, 74, 132
  Hague, William 14
  Hailsham, Lord 9, 165–6, 174
  Heath, Edward 32, 134
  House of Lords 6, 12, 86, 91–2,
    95, 97
  hung parliaments 133–4
  Labour Government 38, 54
  leadership elections 132
  legal services 169
  MacMillan, Harold 132, 133
  Major, John 9, 13–14, 119, 122
  ministers 167
  Prime Minister 131
  referenda 36
  reform 163
  selection process 66, 69
  UK Constitution 13–14
Constitution Unit 43–4
Constitutional Commission for the
    UK 30–7
  civil rights 158
  coalition 32–3

composition 30, 125
Conservative Party 32
constitutional conventions 31
constitutional propriety 125
costs, of 33, 169–70
declaratory role 31, 33
democracy 82
Department of Law 169–70
elections 34–5, 81–2
government 30
House of Commons 34–5
Labour Government 33–4, 36
Members of Parliament 34–6
ministers 125
Northern Ireland 31–2
public consultation 30–1, 32
Queen 141
referenda 35–6
reform 30
role 30–1, 34
royal prerogative. 107
constitutional conventions 27–8, 31,
    137–8
constitutional law:
  Law Commission 20–1
  ministers 162
  Supreme Court 180
constitutions *see also* Australian con-
    stitution, constitutional law, UK
    Constitution:
  Conservative Party 5, 13–14
  France 3–4
  Labour Party 5, 13
  legislation 9–10
  Northern Ireland 20
  role 4
  Royal Commission 22
  unwritten 1–9
  written 1–7, 12
consultation 17–18
  Constitutional Commission for the
      UK 30–1, 32
  Government 22–3
  Labour Government 40

Prime Minister 18
conventions 27–8, 31, 137–8
Counsellors of State 142
Cripps, Stafford 148–9
Crossman, Richard 95, 110
Crown *see also* Queen, royal
    prerogative:
  constitutional monarchy 126–30
  head of state 127–9
  republicanism 127
Crown Appointments Commission
    113–14

democracy:
  citizenship 57–8
  coalitions 78
  Constitutional Commission of the
      UK 82
  elections 60–5, 68–70, 73–82
  failings 56–68
  governments 24–5, 56–9
  head of state 128
  House of Commons 56–9, 82–4
  House of Lords 56, 90
  Labour Government 39
  legitimacy 57
  Members of Parliament 57–74, 78
  Parliamentary 56–8
  parliamentary privilege 73
  Prime Minister 61–2
  proportional representation 62,
      74–9, 127–8
  Queen 56, 130, 139–40
  reform 68–82
  sovereignty 56–8
  whips 66–8, 72–3, 78
departmental committees of inquiry
    17, 23
Department of Law 168–71, 176
devolution 6–7, 13
  Joint Consultative Committee on
      Constitutional Reform 46–7, 51
  Labour Government 38–40, 42,
      52–3, 55

devolution (*cont.*):
  proportional representation 7
  referenda 52–3
  Supreme Court 180
Dicey, A.V. 14, 144

economic policy 117–18, 120
elections *see also* electoral law, pro-
    portional representation
  alternative vote 80–1
  Australia 80–1
  cabinet 116–17, 121
  Conservative Party 63, 64, 74, 132
  Constitutional Commission for the
    UK 34–5, 81–2
  democracy 60–5, 68–70, 73–82
  electoral law 7, 18–19, 25
  first-past-the-post 60–5, 74–8
  France 79–80
  governments 59
  House of Commons 83–4
  House of Lords 89, 99
  Joint Consultative Committee on
    Constitutional Reform 47
  Labour Government 41
  Labour Party 63, 64, 74, 132
  Liberal Democrats 63, 64, 74
  Members of Parliament 68–73
  Parliament 113–15
  party leadership 132
  Prime Minister 114–17, 132–3
  Queen 140
  second-ballot system 79–81
  shadow 111
  Thatcher, Margaret 64
elective dictatorship 9–10, 38–9
entrenchment:
  Bill of Rights 148–59
  European Convention on Human
    Rights 49, 149–50
  legislation 153–6
European Convention on Human
    Rights:
  Bill of Rights 153

cabinet 162
civil rights 145–9, 159–60
  enforcement 159
  entrenchment 49, 149–50
  House of Lords 160
  Human Rights Bill 159
  Human Rights Commission 50
  interpretation 160
  Joint Consultative Committee on
    Constitutional Reform 49–50
  judiciary 159–60
  Labour Government 12, 38, 41,
    49–50, 52–3, 55, 148–9
  Labour Party 149–50
  legislation: compatibility with 149;
    updating by 160
  Liberal Democrats 12–13, 147
  schedules 153

Finland 75
France 3–4
freedom of information 50, 53, 55
freedom of speech 67, 73

GCHQ 124–5
Germany 75–6, 77
government *see also* cabinet, Labour
    Government, ministers,
    Parliament:
  civil rights 144–5, 148, 156
  coalitions 5–6, 32–3, 138–9
  consultation 22–3
  democracy 24–5, 56–9
  Department of Law 168–71, 176
  elections 59
  hung parliament 135
  inquiries 25
  judiciary 172
  law reform 168–71
  minority 134–7
  powers 10–12
  Prime Minister 136
  proportional representation 76–7
  reform 163

Greater London Council 16
Gulf war 122–3

Hague, William 14
Hailsham, Lord 9, 165–6, 174
heads of state 127–9
Heath, Edward 32, 134
Home Office 164–8, 170
House of Commons 9–11; *see also*
    Members of Parliament:
  civil rights 156
  Constitutional Commission for the
    UK 34–5
  democracy 56–9, 82–4
  elections 83–4
  House of Lords 88, 97
  Labour Government 82–3
  Leader of the Opposition 83
  Lord Chancellor's Department 164
  ministers 167, 181–2
  Opposition 83
  Prime Minister 10–11, 109
  reform 82–4
  representative 64–5, 72
  second chambers 153–4
  Select Committee on the
    Modernization of the House of
    Commons 82–3
  sovereignty 154
House of Lords:
  abolition 86, 95
  advantages 93–4
  attendance 91, 100–1
  Bill of Rights 151, 153, 158–61
  civil rights 160–1
  composition 90–1, 98–101
  Conservative Party 6, 12, 86, 91–2,
    95, 97
  cross-benchers 91–2, 97–8
  debates 90
  democracy 56, 90
  elections 88, 99
  European Convention on Human
    Rights 160

  functions 89–92
  hereditary peers 86, 87, 89, 91,
    93–4, 100, 100–2
  House of Commons 88, 94, 97
  joint committee 86–7
  Joint Consultative Committee on
    Constitutional Reform 48, 51
  judiciary 100, 178–80
  Labour Government 41–2, 53, 55,
    85–7, 91–7
  Labour Party 6, 12, 22
  lawyers, in 100
  legislation 88, 89–93, 95–8, 153
  Liberal Democrats 48, 86, 95–7
  life peers 86, 87, 93–4, 97–9
  Ministers 101
  Prime Minister 94, 114
  Public Appointments Unit 99
  public opinion 88
  reduction in powers 98–102
  reform 6, 11–12, 18, 85–102
  select committee 101
  Senate 95–7
  Supreme Court 178–9
  Thatcher, Margaret 95, 114
  veto 160–1
  whips 92
human rights *see* Bill of Rights, civil
    rights, European Convention on
    Human Rights
hung parliaments 5, 131, 133–7, 141

inquiries 25
Institute of Public Policy Research
    12
interception of communications
    107–8
Ireland 75

Joint Consultative Committee on
    Constitutional Reform:
  Bill of Rights 49, 50
  composition 45
  decentralization 46

Joint Consultative Committee on
　　Constitutional Reform (*cont.*):
　devolution 46–7, 51
　elections 47–8
　European Convention on Human
　　Rights 49–50
　freedom of information 50
　House of Lords 48, 51, 96
　Labour Government 45–54
　Liberal Democrats 45–51
　proportional representation 47–8
　public participation 51
　second chambers 96
　terms of reference 45
judicial review 105, 124
judiciary 12; *see also* judicial review:
　accountability 166
　appointments 40, 55, 112–13, 114,
　　172–8, 180–1
　Australian Constitution 29, 52
　background 181
　Bill of Rights 148, 152, 154–5,
　　157–8, 161
　cabinet 173
　career structure 172–5
　Circuit Judicial Committee 175–7
　civil rights 146–8, 157
　complaints 174, 176
　Department of Law 176
　discrimination 173–4
　equal opportunities 174
　European Convention on Human
　　Rights 159–60
　government 172
　House of Lords 100, 178–80
　independence 155, 171–5, 178, 181
　Judicial Services Commission
　　174–7, 180–1
　Judicial Studies Board 178
　Labour Government 40, 52, 55, 175
　Law Secretary 171, 177–8
　legislation 154–5, 178, 179
　Liberal Democrats 174–5
　Lord Chancellor 164–78

　lower 177
　magistrates 175, 177
　ministers 105, 168, 171–3, 175,
　　179, 181–2
　oaths 154
　Parliament 172
　Prime Minister 112–13, 114,
　　172–3, 175
　Privy Council 158, 179, 180
　promotions 176–7
　recorders 177–8
　removal 174–5
　resignation 176
　salaries 171, 172
　separation of powers 179
　solicitors 173
　Supreme Court 178–82
　tenure 174–5
　Thatcher, Margaret 173
　training 178
　UK Constitution 171

Labour Government:
　administration of justice 40
　Bill of Rights 39
　Blair, Tony 9–10, 41, 47, 64, 119,
　　122
　cabinet 111
　Charter of Rights 39, 41, 148
　civil rights 148–9
　Conservative Party 54
　consultation 40
　Cripps, Stafford 148–9
　Crossman, Richard 95, 110
　democracy 39
　devolution 38, 39–40, 42, 52–3, 55
　electoral reform 7
　European Convention on Human
　　Rights 12, 38, 41, 49–50, 52–3,
　　55, 148–9
　freedom of information 52–3, 55
　House of Commons 82–3
　House of Lords 41–2, 53, 55,
　　85–7, 91–5, 97

influences 42–4
Joint Consultative Cabinet
   Committee 53, 54
Joint Consultative Committee on
   Constitutional Reform 45–54
judiciary 40, 52, 55, 175
Liberal Democrat 44–51, 53
Ministry of Legal Administration
   40
Northern Ireland 40
Prime Minister 111, 132
proportional representation 7, 78–9
referenda 36
reform 162
UK Constitution 38–55
voting system 41
Wilson, Harold 110, 132
written constitution 42
Labour Party *see also* Labour
   Government:
Bill of Rights 148–50
Constitutional Commission for the
   UK 33–4
Constitution Unit 43–4
constitutions 5, 13
elections 63, 64, 74, 132
European Convention on Human
   Rights 149–50
House of Lords 6, 12, 22
hung parliaments 133–7
influences, on 42–4
Joint Consultative Cabinet
   Committee 19, 22
leadership elections 132
Lord Chancellor 167
Meet the Challenge: Make the
   Change 38–9, 40
ministerial responsibility 166–7
New Agenda for Democracy, A
   41–2, 52
royal prerogative 106
Scottish Constitutional Convention
   43–4
selection process 65–6, 69

Smith, John 41
Law Commission:
constitutional law 20–21
legislation 20
Lord Chancellor 165
royal prerogative 106–7, 120
Law Reform Committee 20
Law Secretary 169–71, 177–8
legislation:
Bill of Rights 153; incompatibility
   with 152; overriding 160
cabinet 170
civil rights 146–7, 156–7
Conservative Party 9–10
entrenchment 153–6
European Convention on Human
   Rights: compatibility with 149;
   updating, by 160
House of Lords 88, 89–95, 97–8,
   153
judiciary 154–5, 178, 179
Law Commission 20
Law Reform Committee 20
precedents 157
royal prerogative 103–4
second chambers 96, 153–4
subordinate 98
UK Constitution 150–1
legitimacy:
democracy 57
head of state 128
Members of Parliament 57–8
second chambers 96
Liberal Democrats:
Bill of Rights 49, 147–8
coalitions 134–5
elections 63, 64, 74
European Convention on Human
   Rights 12–13, 147
House of Lords 48, 86, 95–8
Joint Consultative Cabinet
   Committee 53
Joint Consultative Committee on
   Constitutional Reform 45–51

Liberal Democrats (*cont.*):
  Judicial Services Commission
    174–5
  ministers 166
  Ministry of Justice 166
  Parliament, dissolution 115–16
  proportional representation 47,
    76–7
  referenda 36
  reform 162–3
  second chambers 95–6
  selection process 66, 69
  Senate 95–8
life peers 86, 87, 93–4, 97–9
Lord Chancellor 164–78

MacMillan, Harold 131, 133
magistrates 175, 177
Major, John 9, 13–14, 119, 122
manifestos 16
Members of Parliament *see also* cabi-
    net, ministers:
  accountability 59, 72
  Constitutional Commission for the
    UK 34–6
  crossing the floor 71–2
  democracy 57–74, 78
  deselection 59–60
  elections 68–73
  freedom of speech 67, 73
  independents 65, 70
  legitimacy 57–8
  local views 71
  loyalty 66–7
  personal lives 71
  recall 70–3
  referenda 34–5
  safe seats 60, 64, 72–3
  selection 59–60, 65–74
  whips 66–7, 68, 72
ministers *see also* cabinet, Prime
    Minister:
  accountability 163–4
  civil rights 146–7

Conservative Party 167
Constitutional Commission of the
    UK 125
constitutional impropriety 124–5
constitutional law 162
Department of Law 167–71
Home Office 164–8, 170
House of Commons 167–8, 181–2
House of Lords 101
informal groups 118–19
judicial review 105
judiciary 105, 168, 171–3, 175,
    179, 181–2
Labour Party 166–7
law reform 163–8
Law Secretary 169–71
legal affairs 163–8
legislation 103–4
Liberal Democrats 166
Lord Chancellor 164–78
Ministerial Code 119
passports 124
powers 103–25
public appointments 113
reform 162, 166–7
reshuffles 108, 110–12
royal prerogative 103–8, 124
safeguards 104–5, 107–8
Ministry of Justice 168
Ministry of Legal Administration 40
Mitterand, François 4
monarchy *see* Crown, Queen
MPs *see* Members of Parliament

Northern Ireland 20, 31–2, 40, 75

Parliament *see also* House of
    Commons, House of Lords,
    Members of Parliament, minis-
    ters, Parliamentary committees,
    parliamentary privilege:
  armed conflict 123
  cabinet 116
  civil rights 148, 150, 156, 157

coalitions 5
constitutional conventions 137–8
democracy 56–84
dissolution 6, 114–16, 137–8; cabinet 116; Queen 139–40
elections 114–15
fixed-term 115–16
hung 5, 131, 133–7, 141
judiciary 172
Liberal Democrats 115–16
Prime Minister 114–16, 137–8
Queen 131, 139–40
second chambers 153–4
sovereignty 57, 150, 153–4, 156
treaties and conventions 123–4
war 123
Parliamentary committees 19
parliamentary privilege 73
passports 124
political parties *see* Conservative Party, Labour Party, Liberal Democrats
prerogative 73
Prime Minister 8–9; *see also* Thatcher, Margaret:
armed conflict 109
Benn, Tony 109
Blair, Tony 9–10, 41, 47, 64, 119, 122
Cabinet 109, 110–25
caretakers 133
Church of England 112, 113–14
civil service 112, 114
coalitions 136–9
Conservative Party 131
constitutional reviews 19
consultation 18
democracy 61–2
economic policy 117–18
elections 114–17, 132–3
government: minority 136–7
Heath, Edward 32, 134
House of Commons 10–11, 109
House of Lords 94, 114

hung parliament 134, 137–8
judiciary 112–13, 114, 172–3, 175
Labour Government 111, 132
MacMillan, Harold 132, 133
Major, John 9, 13–14, 119, 122
Parliament: dissolution 114–16
patronage 110–14
powers 108–21, 125
public appointments 112–14
Queen 126, 131–2, 134, 137–8
reshuffles 108, 110–12
review 125
royal prerogative 103, 109, 120
Wilson, Harold 110, 132
Prince of Wales 141–2
Privy Council:
Bill of Rights 158
Judicial Committee 159, 179, 180
Supreme Court 179, 180
talks on Privy Council terms 18
proportional representation:
additional member system 75–6, 77
Australia 75
coalitions 78
democracy 62, 74–9, 127–8
devolution 7
Finland 75
Germany 75–6, 77
governments 76–7
Ireland 75
Joint Consultative Committee on Constitutional Reform 47–8
Labour Government 7, 78–9
Liberal Democrats 47, 76–7
Northern Ireland 75
referendum 78–9
regional lists system 74–5
single transferable vote 74–5
public appointments 112–14

Queen *see also* Crown, royal prerogative:
coalitions 134, 136

Queen (*cont.*):
  Constitutional Commission of the
    UK 141
  continuity 141–3
  Counsellors of State 142
  criticisms 127
  democracy 56, 130, 139–40
  elections 140
  function 126–7, 129–30, 139–40
  Parliament 131; dissolution 139–40
  political crises 134–5
  popularity 129–30
  Prime Minister 126, 131–2, 134,
    137–8
  Prince of Wales 141–3
  regency 142–3
  republicanism 127
  royal family 127, 130
  royal prerogative 126
  sovereignty 56
  veto 140

recall power 70–3
recorders 177, 178
referenda:
  Conservative Party 36
  Constitutional Commission for the
    UK 36
  devolution 52–3
  Labour Government 36
  Liberal Democrats 36
  Members of Parliament 35–6
  proportional representation 78–9
  Switzerland 36
  United States 36
regency 142–3
regional lists system 74–5
republicanism 126–30
rights *see* civil rights
Royal Commissions 17, 22
royal family 127, 130
royal prerogative:
  armed conflict 122–3
  cabinet 120, 122–3

Constitutional Commission of the
  UK 107
interception of communications
  107–8
judicial review 105, 124
Labour Party 106
Law Commission 106–7, 120
legislation 103
ministers 103–8, 124
passports 124
Prime Minister 103
Queen 126
review 105–8
  Prime Minister 109
safeguards 106–7, 122
sovereignty 123–4
war 122–3

Scotland 26, 43–4; *see also* devolution
second-ballot system 79–81
second chambers 85–102; *see also*
    House of Lords:
  elections 96
  House of Commons 153–4
  Joint Consultative Committee on
    Constitutional Reform 96
  legislation 96, 153–4
  legitimacy 96
  Liberal Democrats 95–6
  parliamentary sovereignty 153–4
  Senate 95–8
  veto 153–4
select committees 19–20, 25–6
  Bill of Rights 158–9
  Department of Law 171
  House of Commons 82–3
  House of Lords 101
separation of powers 179
single transferable vote 74–5
Smith, John 41
sovereignty:
  Bill of Rights 150
  cabinet 123–4
  citizenship 58

civil rights 150, 156
democracy 56–8
House of Commons 154
parliamentary 57, 150, 153–4, 156
royal prerogative 123–4
Queen 56
second chambers 153–4
treaties and conventions 123–4
Speaker's Conferences 18–19, 25
statutes *see* legislation
Supreme Court 178–82
Switzerland 36

Thatcher, Margaret:
armed conflict 109
authoritarianism, of 8–10
cabinet 116–17, 119, 121–2
civil rights 145
civil service 112
election victory 64
elective dictatorship 38–9
House of Lords 95, 114
judiciary 173
reshuffles 110
resignation 122, 132
UK Constitution 9, 13, 54
treaties and conventions 123–4

UK Constitution:
ad hoc changes 23–4

attitudes, towards 8
Bill of Rights 150–1
Conservative Party 13–14
Constitutional Commission 30–6
constitutional monarchy 129–30
head of state 128–9
judiciary 171
Labour Government 38–55
law reform 166
legislation 150–1
President 128–9
Royal Commission 22
Thatcher, Margaret 9, 13, 54
written 1–7, 12, 42
United States 36

voting system *see* elections

Wales *see* devolution
war 109, 122–3
whips:
democracy 66–7, 68, 72–3, 78
House of Lords 92
Members of Parliament 66–7, 68, 72
parliamentary privilege 73
Wilson, Harold 110, 132